SUPPERS AND SNACKS

SUPPERS AND SNACKS

Carol Bowen

CONTENTS

First published in 1984 by Octopus Books Ltd
59 Grosvenor Street, London W1

© 1984 Hennerwood Publications Ltd

ISBN 0 86273 133 X

Printed in England
by Severn Valley Press Ltd

INTRODUCTION

Do not be misled into the belief that you cannot eat well mid-week or weekends unless you spend a great deal of time in the kitchen. It simply isn't true. For today with the introduction of many labour-saving pieces of equipment, convenience-style foods and many beautiful ranges of freezer-to-oven-to-table ware (which saves on valuable washing-up time too!) it is possible to cook delicious, home-made meals in a fraction of the time it used to take. With this in mind you'll see that the preparation time in each of these recipes is kept to a minimum.

Preparing quick, tasty and, moreover, nourishing suppers and snacks does not necessarily demand a mammouth supply of frozen, dried or canned convenience foods. Quite the contrary, it involves judiciously using a few of these alongside fresh ingredients to save time, add flavour or reduce the workload. A well-stocked, not heavily-stocked storecupboard can prove to be the saving grace when unexpected guests call, when a meal for 4 suddenly has to expand to serve 6 and when instant but interesting snacks are required.

Such foods fall into three main categories: dried, canned or bottled, and chilled or frozen.

Dried Storecupboard Standbys: Be generous with your supply of dried herbs, spices and seasonings – they can literally lift a dish from the ordinary to the luxury class. Stock cubes are a must – especially if you haven't the time to make stock, but choose a brand with a natural not overwhelming flavour.

A good selection of dried fruits and nuts will always come in handy. If not as a basic ingredient then certainly as a garnish. Currants, raisins, sultanas, walnuts, almonds, hazelnuts and pine nuts are a good selection to begin with.

An imaginative storecupboard will also stock a good selection of rice, cereals, flour and pasta shapes, perhaps quick bread and pastry mixes, a packet of prepared suet, a can of dried milk to cope with emergencies and a favourite packet of dried soup. Beyond that the choice is yours – dried vegetables such as mushrooms and onions, instant potato and dried peas and beans can all prove useful and tasty if you have time for their preparation.

Canned and Bottled Storecupboard Standbys: These really can prove a bonus – especially since many on the market today give a home-made flavour and texture. Include a good selection of condensed and ordinary soups in your storecupboard – they can substitute for a home-made stock when time is short. A few cans of fish – sardines, anchovies, crab, prawns, mussels and tuna are useful as hors d'oeuvres, in salads or gratin-type dishes. Canned pâté, ham, corned beef, frankfurters, beans, sweetcorn, cook-in sauces, mushrooms, apricots, bottled olives, capers, jam, herrings and chutneys all have a well earned place. Arguably the most useful must be canned tomatoes – skinning, seeding and chopping tomatoes can be a tiresome chore.

Alongside your canned and bottled store must come a good selection of oils, vinegars, salad dressings and, of course, wines, spirits and liqueurs, to add a flavour all their own. A carton of long life milk and one of cream can also prove very handy.

Chilled and Frozen Food Standbys: A refrigerator and freezer must come high on the list of invaluable kitchen assets. A refrigerator can be well-stocked with eggs, milk, butter and cooking fats, bacon, a selection of hard and soft cheeses, a carton or two of fruit juice, a few fresh oranges and lemons and perhaps some ready-made pastry.

The range of prepared frozen foods is extensive and the choice an individual one. However, those foods particularly useful for preparing the recipes in this book include fish fillets or portions, a good-quality minced beef, some ready-made pancakes stacked between foil or freezer paper, a batch of home-made or bought pastry dough, a large bag of fresh breadcrumbs, a good selection of home or commercially-frozen vegetables and fruits and a few standby basics like ready-made hamburgers, a baked flan or pastry case, boil-in-the-bag fish in sauce, chicken joints or pieces, one or two favourite sauces and perhaps an ice cream, mousse or gâteau to add the finishing touch to a home-made family meal. Oddments such as chopped herbs, lemon rind and juice, ends of wine bottles, and a few croûtons come in handy too.

When cooking food for the freezer, reheating ready-made dishes or defrosting frozen foods it is important to follow strict rules on hygiene, as for all cooking. Remember that freezing does not destroy bacteria in foods so some foods like poultry and game birds, pork and sausagemeat and most shellfish items must always be fully thawed and fully cooked to a high temperature before being served. Leftovers should always be stored in the refrigerator (rather than left out in a room) then thoroughly reheated – always aim

to use leftovers within 24 hours. If in any doubt about the freshness of a food then do not eat it.

A Nutritious Eating Plan

Eating snacks need not play havoc with good eating habits. A balanced and varied diet should provide all the nutrients needed for health, and does not necessarily mean buying expensive specialist foods from health food shops. The recipes in this book have been developed so that you can choose a varied and nutritious range of foods, and put together a sensible overall eating plan. Current nutritional recommendations on which to plan include:

★ eating lean meat a maximum of once a day.
★ eating more fish and poultry.
★ not eating too many eggs per week.
★ in general replacing full-fat foods with low-fat alternatives such as skimmed milk, cottage cheese, and low-fat yogurt.
★ eating a wide selection of fruit and vegetables – at least 3 good portions daily.
★ eating more cereals, especially wholemeal varieties.
★ cutting down on *all* fats but especially saturated fats.
★ generally trying to eat less salt and refined sugar.

Helpful Equipment

So much for food in the kitchen – but most cooks have a favourite kitchen appliance they would not live without. It may fit in well with their lifestyle by speeding up the preparation process, cook extra fast, or cut down, or dispense, with any other laborious procedure. The appliances below are especially appropriate to cooking suppers and snacks, although not essential for preparing these recipes.

Mixers, Blenders and Food Processors: It is hard to remember the time when cream was laboriously whipped by hand, breadcrumbs or nuts grated near to the knuckles, and fruit and vegetables puréed with a wooden spoon and sieve; the reason being the valued introduction of mixers, blenders and food processors. Some of the more sophisticated models slice salad vegetables, peel potatoes, shred vegetables, make pasta, sausages, bread and pastry.

Contact Grills: These ingenious little countertop appliances have a variety of uses that defies their size. Not only will they grill steaks, kebabs and fish but also cook instant toasted sandwiches, pizzas and pies, bake biscuits, scones and waffles, cook hamburgers, bacon, chops and small pieces of chicken, pancakes, crêpes and vegetables in foil. For the very best results always follow the manufacturer's instructions.

Microwave Cookers: A microwave cooker is a splendidly flexible piece of equipment for the busy cook who needs to prepare suppers and snacks quickly, efficiently and tastily. It will cook in minutes rather than hours, defrost foods quickly (at a moment's notice), and reheat leftovers. Always follow the manufacturer's instructions.

The Crafty Cook

Despite the help of convenience foods and modern equipment there are still moments in a cook's life when there simply doesn't seem enough time to produce a dazzling meal. Everyone appreciates the difficulty in preparing one mouthwatering meal after another.

Thankfully there are a few clever ideas that the cook can keep up her sleeve for spicing up the simplest of meals so that they need never become humdrum. For example:

★ liven up a stuffing mix (if you haven't the time to make a home-made one from scratch) by substituting half of the water required with a fruit juice or cider. Good flavour combinations include sage and onion with apple or orange juice or cider and thyme and lemon with grapefruit juice.

★ just a spoonful of cream or top of the milk added to a sauce or to pan juices produces that swirl of luxury on plain fried or grilled foods.

★ you can make delicious and unusual short crust pastry if you bind or mix the rubbed-in ingredients with chopped nuts, grated fruit rinds, ground spices, herbs, wheatgerm, chopped cooked bacon, chopped cooked onion, dried coconut and fruit juices to ring the changes.

★ savoury rice recipes taste all the more delicious if you substitute some of the cooking water with fruit juice or stock. Creamed coconut rice also makes a delicious accompaniment with a curry or spiced dish. Add approximately 25 g (1 oz) creamed coconut to 225 g (8 oz) rice, and cook in the usual way.

★ a good choice of marinades helps to tenderize and add flavour to the dullest of meats prior to cooking. Regardless of meat size from kebab cube to man-size pot-roast try this basic marinade. Mix 2 tablespoons vinegar, 1 tablespoon olive oil, ½ teaspoon clear honey, ½ teaspoon dried marjoram and 4 tablespoons apple juice. Marinate the meat for at least 4 hours or, preferably, overnight.

★ ring the changes in traditional stews and casseroles by adding flavoured dumplings 20 minutes before the end of the cooking time. Fruit, herb, spice or bacon-flavoured dumplings are firm favourites. Alternatively, top a stew or casserole with savoury scones or choux buns for a hearty meal in one pot.

★ plain grills can seem most unappetizing but not if they are basted with a flavoursome mixture during cooking. Try barbecue, mustard or marmalade bastes for enviable results.

For a mustard baste, blend together 1 tablespoon wine vinegar, 1 tablespoon made mustard and 50 g (2 oz) soft brown sugar.

For a barbecue baste, blend together 1 tablespoon made mustard, 2 teaspoons soft brown sugar, 1 tablespoon wine vinegar and 1 tablespoon tomato ketchup.

For a marmalade baste, blend 2 tablespoons marmalade, 2 teaspoons soya sauce and 1 tablespoon orange juice.

★ grilled or fried meats and fish, and poached fish, without a sauce or gravy appreciate the addition of a delicious flavoured butter. Have a few ready-made butters in the refrigerator or freezer for speedy use. Use to top jacket potatoes and spread sandwiches too. Herbs like parsley, chives, thyme and tarragon are versatile, or try onion butter, blue cheese butter, mint butter and lemon butter.

★ salads needn't be mournful mouthfuls of rabbit-like food if you combine an imaginative selection of everyday as well as exotic fruits and vegetables with fish, meats, eggs, cheese and often more importantly, a tasty dressing. A screw-topped jar of bulk-made vinaigrette will lend a helping hand when you need it most. Store in the refrigerator and simply shake to use. Flavoursome mayonnaises also store reasonably well if chilled. Try a curried, minted, lemon, garlic or chilli mayonnaise.

★ canned and packet soups offer tremendous advantages to the busy cook. Use them instead of stock for stews, casseroles, chowders and in ready-made dishes such as chilli con carne, shepherd's pie and spaghetti bolognese.

With a swirl of cream, sprinkling of croûtons or topping of onion rings, paprika or herbs they also make beautiful beginnings to any meal.

★ finally remember to serve food with panache by adding attractive garnishes. Mix and match foods with the following garnish ideas: chopped or sprigs of herbs; slices or decorative shapes of tomato and hard-boiled egg; slices, twists, butterflies or wedges of lemon and cucumber; a dusting of spices or coconut; chopped, halved or whole nuts, olives and dried fruit; bunches of cress, mint and watercress; a border of shredded lettuce or Chinese cabbage; a scattering of crispy croûtons; set foods in a golden brown border of piped then grilled mashed potato; top with a spoonful or swirl of soured cream, whipped cream or yogurt; garnish with unpeeled shellfish, e.g., prawns or shrimps; glaze cold dishes with glistening aspic and colourful vegetable pieces arranged attractively; serve foods in hollowed-out fruit and vegetable shells; top with toasted French bread, choux buns, cut out scone shapes or freshly cooked fluffy dumplings; sprinkle with cheese or toasted breadcrumbs; serve where appropriate in colourful napkins; garnish with toast fingers or triangles; finish oriental-style with spring onion curls, carrot scrolls or decorative vegetable shapes; top with pleated and grilled bacon rashers; or finally sprinkle with julienne strips of fruit rind like orange, lemon or lime.

SANDWICHES & SIZZLERS

PORK, BEEF AND CHICKEN SATÉ

350 g (12 oz) lean boneless pork
350 g (12 oz) rump steak
350 g (12 oz) boneless chicken breasts, skinned
6 tablespoons oil
6 tablespoons soy sauce
1 garlic clove, peeled and crushed
1 tablespoon curry powder
1½ tablespoons caster sugar

Peanut sauce:
2 tablespoons oil
100 g (4 oz) ground salted peanuts
1 onion, peeled and minced
1 garlic clove, peeled and crushed
1 teaspoon chilli powder
1 teaspoon ground coriander
¼ teaspoon ground cumin
300 ml (½ pint) coconut milk or light chicken stock
2 tablespoons light brown sugar
1 tablespoon soy sauce
1 tablespoon lemon juice

Preparation time: 30 minutes, plus marinating
Cooking time: about 20 minutes

1. Cut the pork, beef and chicken into 1 cm (½ inch) cubes, keeping the meats separate.
2. Mix the oil with the soy sauce, garlic, curry powder and sugar, blending well. Marinate the meats separately in one-third of this marinade for about 4-6 hours. Ⓐ
3. Meanwhile, for the sauce, heat the oil in a pan. Add the peanuts, onion, garlic, chilli powder, coriander and cumin and fry for 2 minutes. Add the coconut milk or stock, sugar, soy sauce and lemon juice. Bring to the boil, lower the heat and simmer for 10 minutes or until creamy. Allow to cool.
4. Thread the meats on to 12 small skewers, using four for each type of meat. (Remember if you intend to use the traditional wooden skewers to soak them in cold water for 30 minutes before they are required.) Brush with a little of the peanut sauce.
5. Place under a preheated hot grill and cook for about 6-8 minutes until browned on all sides. Serve hot with the saté sauce.

Ⓐ The meats can be marinated for up to 24 hours before required if kept in the refrigerator.

GRILLED GREEK PITTA POCKETS

4 slices medium-sized pitta bread
Greek salad
100 g (4 oz) cooked lamb, finely shredded
50 g (2 oz) mushrooms, thinly sliced
1 small bunch spring onions, trimmed and chopped
2 lettuce leaves, shredded
2 tomatoes, skinned, seeded and chopped
4 black olives, stoned and sliced
2-3 tablespoons yogurt salad dressing
salt
freshly ground black pepper
75 g (3 oz) cheese, grated

Preparation time: 20 minutes
Cooking time: 5-6 minutes

1. Carefully cut a slit across the top of each pitta bread but not through to the base. Gently open out the bread pockets each side of the slit.
2. Mix the lamb with the mushrooms, onions, lettuce, tomatoes, olives, dressing and salt and pepper to taste, blending well.
3. Stuff the pitta pockets equally with the Greek salad mixture and place on a grill rack. Sprinkle the cheese on top.
Place under a preheated moderate grill and cook for about 5-6 minutes until golden and bubbly. Serve at once whole or cut through into halves.

Variation:
Slices of pitta bread can also be filled with a West Indian mixture of ingredients. Stuff the pitta pockets with 100 g (4 oz) cooked diced chicken mixed with 50 g (2 oz) finely chopped pineapple, 50 g (2 oz) finely chopped green pepper, 1 small sliced banana, 25 g (1 oz) toasted almonds, 2-3 tablespoons mayonnaise and salt and pepper to taste. Top with the cheese and grill as above.

Pork, beef and chicken saté with peanut sauce served separately; Grilled Greek pitta pockets

SALAMI AND MOZZARELLA SNACK TOASTS

4 thick slices Farmhouse crusty bread
100 g (4 oz) salami, rinded and thinly sliced
4 tomatoes, skinned and sliced
salt
freshly ground black pepper
1 green or yellow pepper, cored, seeded and sliced
75 g (3 oz) Mozzarella cheese, thinly sliced
1 teaspoon dried mixed herbs
4-8 small black olives
To garnish:
sprigs of parsley

Preparation time: 15 minutes
Cooking time: about 10 minutes

1. Place the bread under a preheated hot grill and toast until golden on one side.
2. Turn the bread slices over and cover with the salami and tomatoes, adding salt and pepper to taste.
3. Top with the pepper slices and cheese. Sprinkle with the herbs, place under a preheated moderate grill and toast for about 10 minutes until cooked through and bubbly.
4. Serve hot, topped with the black olives and garnished with sprigs of parsley.

MEXICAN BEANFEAST SNACK

1 × 450 g (1 lb) can baked beans in tomato sauce
1-2 teaspoons chilli seasoning
1 canned pimiento, finely chopped
½ teaspoon Worcestershire sauce
50 g (2 oz) butter
6 eggs, beaten
salt
freshly ground black pepper
4 slices hot buttered toast
4 tomatoes, thinly sliced
To garnish:
sprigs of Continental parsley

Preparation time: 10 minutes
Cooking time: 10-15 minutes

1. Place the beans in a pan. Add the chilli seasoning, pimiento and Worcestershire sauce, blending well. Heat gently until very hot.
2. Meanwhile, melt the butter in a pan. Add the eggs with salt and pepper to taste and cook, over a gentle heat, until lightly scrambled.
3. Spoon the scrambled egg around the edges of the prepared toast.
4. Spoon the bean mixture into the centre of the egg 'nests'. Top with tomato slices and garnish with sprigs of parsley. Serve at once.

BAKED CONTINENTAL LOAF

1 large long crusty loaf
50 g (2 oz) butter
1 garlic clove, peeled and crushed
8 slices quick-melting cheese
8 slices cooked Continental-style ham
8 slices garlic sausage
2 tomatoes, thinly sliced

Preparation time: 10 minutes
Cooking time: 15-20 minutes
Oven: 190°C, 375°F, Gas Mark 5

1. Make eight crosswise cuts equally along the length of the loaf almost to the base.
2. Cream the butter with the garlic and spread thinly between the slices of bread.
3. Place one slice of cheese, ham, garlic sausage and tomato in each cut. Press gently together to re-form the loaf shape.
4. Cover the loaf loosely with foil. Place in a preheated oven and cook for 10-15 minutes.
5. Remove the top of the foil and cook for a further 5 minutes or until golden and bubbly. Pull apart or cut between the slices of bread to serve.

Spread each of the cuts with creamed butter.

Insert the cheese, ham, garlic sausage and tomato.

Salami and Mozzarella snack toasts; Mexican beanfeast snack; Baked Continental loaf

SNACK SLICES

Serves 2
4 slices Danish rye bread
50 g (2 oz) butter
4 lettuce leaves
4 slices salami, rinded
2 tablespoons grated white cabbage
1 tablespoon grated carrot
2 spring onions, trimmed and chopped
4 hard-boiled eggs, shelled and chopped
2 tablespoons garlic mayonnaise
salt
freshly ground black pepper
1 teaspoon capers
2 sausages, grilled and sliced
2 tablespoons mayonnaise
1 teaspoon mango chutney
1 teaspoon sultanas
1 tomato, sliced
2 tablespoons mustard and cress

Preparation time: 25 minutes

By increasing the quantities, you can make these especially good for a lunch or supper party.

1. Spread the bread generously with the butter and top each slice with a lettuce leaf.
2. Top two of the slices of bread with the salami. Mix the cabbage with the carrot, spring onions, two of the eggs, the garlic mayonnaise and salt and pepper to taste. Spoon on top of the salami and garnish with a few capers.
3. Top the remaining two slices of bread with the sliced sausages. Mix the remaining eggs with the mayonnaise, chutney, sultanas and salt and pepper to taste. Spoon on top of the sausages. Arrange the slices of tomato on top and sprinkle with the mustard and cress.
4. Serve one salami and one sausage snack slice per person.

If you need to make sandwiches and rolls in advance and you don't want them literally to go limp on you, then substitute crisp toast or crispy baked bread for the bread and rolls used in the recipes on this page. Top with butter, margarine or another waterproof coating, such as soft cheese, to serve as a protection to the base from moist fillings and toppings. Cover with cling film or foil to prevent drying out and store in a larder, chiller or refrigerator for freshly-made results.

SPICY CLUB SANDWICH

100 g (4 oz) boned tandoori chicken, cut into bite-sized pieces
4 tablespoons mayonnaise
1 teaspoon mild curry powder
1 tablespoon seedless raisins
4 rashers back bacon, rinded
8 slices brown bread, crusts removed and toasted
4 slices white bread, crusts removed and toasted
50 g (2 oz) butter
4 lettuce leaves
about 16 thin slices cucumber
1 small green pepper, cored, seeded and sliced
2 tomatoes, thinly sliced
1 tablespoon chopped fresh parsley

Preparation time: 30 minutes
Cooking time: 3-5 minutes

1. Mix the tandoori chicken with the mayonnaise, curry powder and raisins, blending well.
2. Place the bacon under a preheated hot grill and cook until crisp. Drain on paper towels.
3. Spread one side of the brown bread and both sides of the white bread with the butter.
4. Spread the chicken mixture equally over four slices of the brown bread. Top each with a slice of white bread.
5. Cover each white slice of bread with a lettuce leaf, four cucumber slices and slices of green pepper.
6. Top each sandwich with a final slice of brown bread. Cover with tomato slices and a rasher of bacon. Sprinkle with chopped parsley and serve. Eat with a knife and fork.

NEW YORKERS

8 slices rye bread
225 g (8 oz) full fat soft cheese
4 slices smoked salmon
1 red onion, peeled and sliced into rings
16 sprigs fresh coriander
freshly ground black pepper

Preparation time: 10-15 minutes

1. Spread the slices of bread thickly with the soft cheese.
2. Cut each slice of smoked salmon in half and roll each into a small cornet shape. Place a smoked salmon cornet on top of each slice of bread.
3. Top each with a few rings of red onion and two sprigs of fresh coriander. Sprinkle with a little freshly ground black pepper and serve.

CLOCKWISE FROM THE LEFT: Union Jack snacks; Snack slices; Spicy club sandwich

UNION JACK SNACKS

4 large soft round rolls topped with sesame seeds
75 g (3 oz) butter
100 g (4 oz) cold roast Scotch beef, shredded
4 tablespoons mayonnaise
1-2 teaspoons creamed horseradish
1 tablespoon snipped fresh chives
4 lettuce leaves
100 g (4 oz) mature English Cheddar cheese, thinly sliced
1 tomato, thinly sliced
2 tablespoons ploughman's or chunky brown pickle
1 medium leek, cleaned and very thinly sliced
1 teaspoon grated lemon rind
1 tablespoon seedless raisins

Preparation time: 25 minutes

1. Cut three horizontal slits in each roll but do not cut through the bread to the other side. Spread the bread layers with the butter.
2. Mix the beef with half of the mayonnaise, the horseradish relish and chives, blending well.
3. Place a lettuce leaf on the bottom layer of each roll and top with an equal quantity of the beef filling.
4. Fill the middle layer of the rolls with slices of cheese, topped with slices of tomato and the pickle.
5. Mix the leek with the lemon rind, remaining mayonnaise and raisins, blending well. Use to fill the top layer of the rolls. Press the top of each roll down lightly before serving.

CROQUE MADAME

100 g (4 oz) back bacon, rinded and cut into half lengthways
8 thin slices white bread, crusts removed
1-2 teaspoons wholegrain mustard
100 g (4 oz) Gruyère cheese, sliced
2 tomatoes, thinly sliced
40 g (1½ oz) butter, melted

Preparation time: 15 minutes
Cooking time: 10-15 minutes
Oven: 230°C, 450°F, Gas Mark 8

1. Place the bacon under a preheated hot grill and cook until crisp. Drain on paper towels.
2. Spread half of the bread slices with mustard to taste. Top each with an equal quantity of cheese, bacon and tomato slices. Cover with the remaining bread slices, pressing down well.
3. Place on a baking sheet and brush lightly with about half of the butter. Place in a preheated oven and cook for about 5 minutes or until lightly browned.
4. Using tongs, turn the sandwiches over and brush with the remaining butter. Bake for a further 3-5 minutes. Cut in half diagonally to serve.

FRENCH BREAD PIZZA TOPPERS

1 large long French stick
3 tablespoons tomato purée
1 × 227 g (8 oz) can tomatoes, drained and chopped
1 teaspoon dried oregano or marjoram
salt
freshly ground black pepper
100 g (4 oz) Cheddar cheese, grated
2 × 50 g (2 oz) cans anchovy fillets in oil, drained
To garnish:
few black olives

Preparation time: 15 minutes
Cooking time: 12-14 minutes

1. Slice the French stick in half horizontally and in length. Place under a preheated hot grill and toast until golden.
2. Spread the two halves of bread with the tomato purée. Top with the tomatoes, herbs, salt and pepper to taste and cheese.
3. Arrange the anchovy fillets in a lattice over the cheese and garnish with the olives.
4. Place under a preheated moderate grill and cook for about 10 minutes until golden and bubbly.
5. Serve hot, cut into thick slices.

Variation:
Use bacon and stuffed green olives instead of anchovies and black olives. Cook 225 g (8 oz) back bacon rashers, under a preheated moderate grill until crisp. Cool then crumble the bacon coarsely. Sprinkle over the tomato base, top with the cheese and garnish with a few sliced stuffed olives. Cook as above.

FOR MICE AND MEN

4 slices wholemeal bread
40 g (1½ oz) butter
4 tomatoes, sliced
salt
freshly ground black pepper
12 canned asparagus spears
100 g (4 oz) Cheshire cheese, grated

Preparation time: 5 minutes
Cooking time: 4-5 minutes

For mice and men; French bread pizza toppers

For mice and men are American toasties that claim to satisfy the smallest to the heartiest appetites!

1. Place the slices of bread under a preheated hot grill and toast until golden on one side.
2. Turn the bread slices over and spread generously with the butter.
3. Top with the tomato slices. Sprinkle with salt and pepper, and add the asparagus spears and cheese.
4. Place under a preheated moderate grill and cook for about 4-5 minutes until golden and bubbly. Serve at once.

INDONESIAN LAMB KEBABS

150 ml (¼ pint) plain unsweetened yogurt
1 teaspoon ground ginger
1 garlic clove, peeled and crushed
¼ teaspoon ground cumin
¼ teaspoon ground coriander
2 tablespoons lemon juice
1 tablespoon oil
salt
freshly ground black pepper
450 g (1 lb) boned shoulder or leg of lamb, cubed
2 medium onions, peeled
1 green pepper, cored, seeded and cut into 8 pieces
1 red pepper, cored, seeded and cut into 8 pieces
12 medium button mushrooms

Preparation time: 20 minutes, plus marinating
Cooking time: 15-20 minutes

1. Mix the yogurt with the ginger, garlic, cumin, coriander, lemon juice, oil and salt and pepper to taste. Add the lamb and toss well. Cover and leave to marinate for 2-3 hours in a cool place. Ⓐ
2. Blanch the onions in boiling water for 3 minutes, then drain. When cool, quarter the onions.
3. Remove the lamb with a slotted spoon and thread on to four skewers, alternating with the onion quarters, pepper pieces and mushrooms.
4. Brush with the marinade. Place under a preheated hot grill and cook for about 15-20 minutes until golden and cooked through. Baste frequently with the marinade during cooking. Serve with boiled rice.

Ⓐ The lamb can be marinated up to 24 hours before required if kept in the refrigerator.

MUSHROOM AND BEEF STROGANOF TOAST TOPPERS

450 g (1 lb) rare roast beef
salt
freshly ground black pepper
25 g (1 oz) butter
2 tablespoons finely chopped onion
175 g (6 oz) button mushrooms, sliced
5 tablespoons mayonnaise
5 tablespoons soured cream
pinch of cayenne pepper
1 tablespoon snipped fresh chives
4 slices wholemeal or rye bread
sprigs of curly endive or watercress

CLOCKWISE FROM THE LEFT: Indonesian lamb kebabs ;
Beef, apricot and apple kebabs ; Mushroom and beef stroganof toast toppers

BEEF, APRICOT AND APPLE KEBABS

450 g (1 lb) beef topside, thinly sliced
25 g (1 oz) butter
1 onion, peeled and chopped
100 g (4 oz) fresh white breadcrumbs
½ teaspoon dried thyme
2 tablespoons chopped fresh parsley
salt
freshly ground black pepper
2 teaspoons lemon juice
1 egg (sizes 1, 2), beaten
1 × 482 g (1 lb 1 oz) can whole apricots, drained, or 12 fresh apricots, skinned and stoned
3 green dessert apples, cored and cut into eighths
4 bay leaves
1 × 375 g (13 oz) can cook-in barbecue sauce

Preparation time: 25 minutes
Cooking time: 25-30 minutes

1. Spread the beef flat and cut into twelve strips about 4 cm (1½ inches wide).
2. Melt the butter in a pan. Add the onion and cook for 5 minutes. Remove from the heat, stir in the breadcrumbs, thyme, parsley and salt and pepper to taste, blending well. Bind together to make a stuffing with the lemon juice and egg. Divide the mixture evenly between the beef strips and roll up.
3. Thread the stuffed beef rolls on to four skewers, alternating with the apricots, apple slices and bay leaves. Brush with the barbecue sauce.
4. Place under a preheated moderate grill and cook for about 20-25 minutes until golden, turning frequently and basting with the barbecue sauce from time to time.
5. Serve hot with any remaining barbecue sauce.

Preparation time: 15 minutes
Cooking time: about 5 minutes

1. Slice the beef across the grain into fairly thick slices. Shred into fine strips about 5 cm (2 inches) long. Season generously with salt and pepper to taste.
2. Melt the butter in a pan. Add the onion and cook for 2 minutes. Add the mushrooms and cook for a further 2 minutes. Remove from the heat and stir in the mayonnaise, cream, cayenne pepper and chives.
3. Place the slices of bread under a preheated hot grill and toast until golden on both sides.
4. Add the beef to the stroganoff mixture and heat for about 1 minute over a very gentle heat. Do not boil.
5. Top the slices of toast with curly endive or watercress and spoon over the stroganof. Serve at once.

Crab gratinée; Plaice and lime pinwheel grills

PLAICE AND LIME PINWHEEL GRILLS

75 g (3 oz) butter, softened
2 tablespoons snipped fresh chives
40 g (1½ oz) fresh white breadcrumbs
grated rind of 1 lime
4 tablespoons lime juice
salt
freshly ground white pepper
8 plaice fillets, skinned
To garnish:
twists of lime
sprigs of dill or fennel

Preparation time: 20 minutes
Cooking time: 10-13 minutes

1. Beat the butter with the chives in a bowl until soft and creamy. Add the breadcrumbs, lime rind and enough lime juice to make a stuffing with a good spreading consistency. Add salt and pepper to taste.
2. Spread the plaice fillets with equal quantities of the stuffing, roll up from the wide end and secure each with a wooden cocktail stick, using a small sharp pointed knife to make an incision if necessary.
3. Place in a greased flameproof gratin dish and sprinkle with the remaining lime juice.
4. Place under a preheated hot grill and cook for 5 minutes. Turn over and grill for a further 5-8 minutes.
5. Serve at once garnished with twists of lime and dill or fennel.

CRAB GRATINÉE

6 crab claws
100 g (4 oz) peeled prawns
40 g (1½ oz) butter
2 tablespoons plain flour
120 ml (4 fl oz) dry white wine
1 tablespoon lemon juice
2 teaspoons chopped fresh parsley
2 tablespoons double cream
½ head Chinese cabbage, shredded
6 tablespoons dried white breadcrumbs
To garnish:
dill leaves or sprigs of parsley

Preparation time: 30 minutes
Cooking time: about 10-15 minutes

1. Crack the crab claws and remove the flesh. Flake or chop coarsely and mix with the prawns.
2. Melt 15 g (½ oz) of the butter in a pan. Add the flour and cook for 1 minute, stirring. Gradually add the wine and lemon juice to make a smooth sauce. Bring to the boil and cook for 1 minute, stirring. Remove from the heat, stir in the parsley and cream, blending well.
3. Meanwhile, melt the remaining butter in a pan. Add the Chinese cabbage and fry quickly for 1-2 minutes or until just softened. Spoon equally into four flameproof dishes or scallop shells. Make a hollow in the centre of each.
4. Fill each hollow with an equal quantity of the crab and prawn mixture and spoon over the sauce.
5. Sprinkle with the breadcrumbs. Place under a pre-heated hot grill for about 2-4 minutes until golden. Serve at once garnished with dill leaves or parsley.

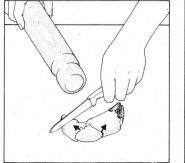

Using a knife and rolling pin, crack the crab claws by hitting them in two places.

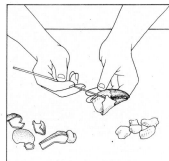

Scoop out the crab flesh with a skewer or the end of a small spoon.

LASAGNE ROMA

225 g (8 oz) green lasagne sheets
1 teaspoon oil
1 recipe Savoury mince (page 69)
1 teaspoon dried oregano
25 g (1 oz) butter
25 g (1 oz) plain flour
300 ml (½ pint) milk
50 g (2 oz) strong Cheddar cheese, grated
1 red pepper, cored, seeded and sliced into rings
2 tablespoons grated Parmesan cheese

Preparation time: 30 minutes
Cooking time: 35-40 minutes

This is a very speedy recipe for lasagne where the finished dish, after cooking the pasta and meat filling, simply needs grilling rather than baking to serve.

1. Cook the lasagne in a pan of lightly salted boiling water with the oil according to the packet instructions for about 10 minutes until tender. Drain thoroughly.
2. Meanwhile, prepare the Savoury mince and heat through until very hot. Stir in the oregano, blending well.
3. Layer the pasta and mince mixture in a greased hot flameproof dish.
4. Melt the butter in a pan. Add the flour and cook for 1 minute, stirring. Gradually add the milk to make a smooth sauce. Bring to the boil and cook for 2-3 minutes, stirring. Add the grated cheese and mix well to blend.
5. Pour over the lasagne mixture. Top with the pepper rings and sprinkle with the Parmesan cheese.
6. Place under a preheated moderate grill and cook for about 10 minutes until golden and bubbly. Serve hot.

Variation:
Lasagne is also delicious layered with a fish and sea-food mixture. Mix 350 g (12 oz) cooked flaked white fish with 100 g (4 oz) peeled prawns, 50 g (2 oz) canned mussels, 300 ml (½ pint) hot thick white sauce, grated rind and juice of 1 lemon, 2 tablespoons chopped fresh parsley and salt and pepper to taste. Layer with the pasta as above, top with the cheese sauce, and pepper rings if wished. Dust with Parmesan cheese and cook under a preheated grill as above.

FROM THE STORE CUPBOARD

HAKE PAPRIKA

75 g (3 oz) butter
2 large onions, peeled and sliced
3 canned pimientos, chopped
4 frozen hake, haddock or whiting portions, thawed
salt
freshly ground black pepper
300 ml (½ pint) plain unsweetened yogurt
2 teaspoons paprika
To garnish:
bread croûtons
sprigs of parsley

Preparation time: 15 minutes
Cooking time: 30-35 minutes
Oven: 190°C, 375°F, Gas Mark 5

1. Melt 50 g (2 oz) of the butter in a frying pan. Add the onions and cook for about 5 minutes until softened. Add the pimientos, mixing well.
2. Spoon half of the onion mixture into a greased ovenproof dish. Top with the fish and sprinkle with salt and pepper to taste. Dot with the remaining butter. Place in a preheated oven and cook, uncovered, for 15 minutes.
3. Top with the remaining onion mixture. Mix the yogurt with the paprika and pour over the fish. Bake for a further 10-15 minutes.
4. Garnish with bread croûtons and parsley sprigs. Serve at once.

HERBY CHEESE PASTA

175 g (6 oz) green or white tagliatelle
100 g (4 oz) cream cheese with herbs and garlic
4 eggs, beaten
225 g (8 oz) streaky bacon, rinded and chopped
1 small onion, peeled and chopped
225 g (8 oz) button mushrooms, sliced
To garnish:
1 tablespoon chopped fresh parsley
1 tomato, cut into wedges

Preparation time: 20 minutes
Cooking time: 20-25 minutes

TOMATO AND TUNA REDSKINS

4 large beef tomatoes
25 g (1 oz) butter
1 onion, peeled and chopped
1×200 g (7 oz) can tuna fish in oil, drained and flaked
75 g (3 oz) fresh white breadcrumbs
1 tablespoon chopped fresh parsley
1 egg (sizes 5, 6), beaten
salt
freshly ground black pepper
1×50 g (2 oz) can anchovy fillets in oil
To garnish:
small black olives
sprigs of Continental parsley

Preparation time: 20 minutes
Cooking time: 30 minutes
Oven: 180°C, 350°F, Gas Mark 4

1. Slice a thin cap from the top of each tomato, scoop out and discard the inner seeds.
2. Melt the butter in a pan. Add the onion and cook for 5 minutes. Remove from the heat, and stir in the tuna, breadcrumbs, parsley, egg, salt and pepper.
3. Spoon the mixture into the prepared tomatoes.
4. Drain the anchovies, reserving the oil, and arrange over the top of the tomatoes. Place in an ovenproof dish and drizzle with the anchovy oil.
5. Cook in a preheated oven for about 20 minutes or until tender. Garnish with black olives, parsley and serve hot with crusty bread.

1. Cook the pasta in a pan of boiling salted water according to the packet instructions for about 8-10 minutes. Drain thoroughly and keep warm.
2. Mix the cream cheese with the eggs and reserve.
3. Meanwhile, fry the bacon in its own fat in a frying pan until crisp and golden. Add the onion and mushrooms and cook for a further 5 minutes.
4. Stir the egg mixture, bacon, onion and mushrooms into the pasta, blending well. Stir over a very gentle heat until the mixture thickens slightly.
5. Spoon into a warmed serving dish and sprinkle with parsley. Top with tomato wedges and serve.

Hake paprika; Tomato and tuna redskins

CHILLI BEEF WITH BEANS

275 g (10 oz) leftover roast beef, cut into thin strips
6 tablespoons orange juice
1 tablespoon lemon juice
2 tablespoons black bean sauce
  or 2 tablespoons beef extract
2 tablespoons chilli seasoning
1 teaspoon cornflour
salt
freshly ground black pepper
3 tablespoons oil
1 large red pepper, cored, seeded and sliced
1 onion, peeled and sliced
1 × 283 g (10 oz) can black-eye beans, drained

Preparation time: 10 minutes, plus marinating
Cooking time: about 10 minutes

1. Mix the beef with the orange juice, lemon juice, black bean sauce or beef extract, chilli seasoning, cornflour and salt and pepper to taste in a bowl. Cover and leave to marinate for 1 hour.
2. Heat the oil in a large frying pan or wok and add the pepper and onion. Stir-fry, over a high heat, for 2-3 minutes.
3. Add the beef and marinade mixture and stir-fry for a further 2 minutes. Add the black-eye beans and stir-fry for a further 1 minute.
4. Serve with cooked Chinese noodles or tagliatelle.

BEEFBURGERS WITH SAUCE CHASSEUR

4 × 100-175 g (4-6 oz) beefburgers or hamburgers
4 thick slices bread, toasted
1 tablespoon chopped fresh parsley
Sauce:
2 tablespoons oil
25 g (1 oz) lean back bacon, rinded and chopped
1 small celery stick, chopped
1 small carrot, peeled and chopped
2 tablespoons flour
150 ml (¼ pint) beef stock
150 ml (¼ pint) dry white wine
1 teaspoon tomato purée
1 teaspoon Dijon mustard
2 large tomatoes, peeled, seeded and chopped
salt
freshly ground black pepper
25 g (1 oz) butter
100 g (4 oz) button mushrooms, chopped
1 small onion, peeled and chopped
2 tablespoons sherry or brandy (optional)

Preparation time: 15 minutes
Cooking time: about 45 minutes

1. For the sauce, heat the oil in a pan. Add the bacon, celery and carrot and cook for about 5 minutes until softened.
2. Add the flour and cook very gently for about 15 minutes or until a rich brown colour. Gradually add the stock and wine, blending well. Stir in the tomato purée, mustard and tomatoes. Cook, over a moderate heat, for 5 minutes.
3. Pass the sauce through a fine sieve, reheat and season with salt and pepper to taste.
4. Meanwhile, melt the butter in a pan. Add the mushrooms and onion and cook for about 5 minutes until softened. Stir into the sauce with the sherry or brandy if used. Keep warm.
5. Meanwhile, place the burgers under a preheated hot grill and cook for about 5-8 minutes each side depending upon size and according to taste.
6. To serve, top each toasted bread slice with a burger and spoon over the sauce. Sprinkle with the parsley and serve. Accompany with grilled tomatoes and mushrooms.

Beefburgers with sauce chasseur; Deep-fried crispy beef and bean pancakes

DEEP-FRIED CRISPY BEEF AND BEAN PANCAKES

225 g (8 oz) lean minced beef
50 g (2 oz) button mushrooms, sliced
2 × 225 g (8 oz) cans curried beans with sultanas
salt
freshly ground black pepper
8 cooked Pancakes (see Seafood pancakes page 33)
25 g (1 oz) butter
1 tablespoon oil
To garnish:
wedges of lemon
sprigs of parsley

Preparation time: 30 minutes
Cooking time: 20-25 minutes

1. Place the beef in a pan and cook, without any extra fat, for about 5 minutes or until lightly browned.
2. Add the mushrooms and cook for a further 5 minutes. Remove from the heat, stir in the beans and salt and pepper to taste.

3. Spoon the beef and bean mixture equally into the centre of each pancake. Fold opposite sides of each pancake in to meet in the centre, and roll the remaining two sides in to enclose the filling completely. Press down gently to seal.
4. Heat the butter and oil in a large frying pan. Add the pancakes and fry over a moderate heat until crisp and golden on both sides. Drain on paper towels.
5. Serve hot, garnished with wedges of lemon and sprigs of parsley.

Fold opposite sides of pancake over filling.

Roll up the remaining two sides and press gently.

DEVILLED SPANISH PIZZA

Base:
225 g (8 oz) self-raising flour
1 teaspoon baking powder
1 teaspoon salt
25 g (1 oz) butter, softened
150 ml (¼ pint) milk
1-2 tablespoons Dijon mustard
Filling:
1 × 800 g (1 lb 12 oz) can tomatoes, drained and chopped
1 onion, peeled and chopped
2 tablespoons tomato purée
2 teaspoons dried oregano
salt
freshly ground black pepper
Topping:
175 g (6 oz) Cheddar or Mozzarella cheese, sliced
100 g (4 oz) salami, chorizo or garlic sausage,
    rinded and sliced
50 g (2 oz) pimiento-stuffed green olives, sliced
1 tablespoon grated Parmesan cheese

Preparation time: 30 minutes
Cooking time: 45 minutes - 1 hour
Oven: 200°C, 400°F, Gas Mark 6

1. For the base, sift the flour with the baking powder and salt into a bowl. Rub in the butter until the mixture resembles fine breadcrumbs. Mix to a soft dough with the milk.
2. Roll out on a lightly floured surface to a 25 cm (10 inch) round and place on a greased baking sheet. Spread with the mustard.
3. Meanwhile for the filling, place the tomatoes, onion, tomato purée and oregano in a pan with salt and pepper to taste. Cook for about 15-20 minutes over a moderate heat, stirring occasionally, until very thick and pulpy. Spoon over the pizza base to within 2.5 cm (1 inch) of the edges.
4. Top with the cheese, salami, chorizo or garlic sausage, olives and Parmesan cheese.
5. Place in a preheated oven and cook for about 30-40 minutes until well risen and golden brown.
6. Serve hot, cut into wedges, with a tossed green salad.

FLUFFY FISH SOUFFLÉ

40 g (1½ oz) butter
25 g (1 oz) plain flour
200 ml (7 fl oz) milk
4 tablespoons double cream
salt
freshly ground white pepper
4 eggs, separated, plus 1 egg white
225 (8 oz) cooked white, smoked or shell fish, skinned,
    boned and flaked
1 tablespoon chopped fresh dill (optional)

Preparation time: 20 minutes
Cooking time: 40 minutes
Oven: 190°C, 375°F, Gas Mark 5

1. Melt the butter in a pan. Add the flour and cook for 1 minute, stirring. Gradually add the milk to make a smooth thick sauce. Bring to the boil and cook for 2-3 minutes, stirring.
2. Remove from the heat, stir in the cream, salt and pepper to taste, and the four egg yolks one by one. Finally, gently stir in the fish.
3. Whisk all five egg whites until they stand in stiff peaks and fold into the fish mixture lightly with a metal spoon.
4. Spoon into a greased 18 cm (7 inch) soufflé dish and sprinkle with the dill if used.
5. Place in a preheated oven and cook for about 35 minutes until well risen, firm and golden.

DUTCH CHEESE FONDUE

300 ml (½ pint) dry white wine or cider
1 garlic clove, peeled and crushed
½ teaspoon ground nutmeg
450 g (1 lb) Gouda or Edam cheese, finely grated
1 tablespoon cornflour
salt
freshly ground black pepper
2-3 tablespoons Kirsch
1 large French stick, cubed

Preparation time: 10 minutes
Cooking time: 10-15 minutes

1. Heat the wine or cider, garlic and nutmeg in a fondue pot or heavy-based saucepan until hot but not boiling.
2. Toss the cheese in the cornflour and add to the wine mixture, a little at a time, stirring very well to dissolve. Cook slowly over a gentle heat until very thick and creamy.
3. Add salt and pepper to taste and stir in the Kirsch.
4. Serve the fondue hot with speared cubes of the French bread. Dip the cubes into the fondue to eat.

BUBBLING EGGS MORNAY

450 g (1 lb) potatoes, peeled
25 g (1 oz) butter
salt
freshly ground black pepper
4 hard-boiled eggs, shelled and halved
Sauce:
40 g (1½ oz) butter
25 g (1 oz) plain flour
300 ml (½ pint) milk
½ teaspoon made mustard
75 g (3 oz) Cheddar cheese, grated
1 tablespoon snipped fresh chives
To garnish:
sprigs of parsley

Preparation time: 30 minutes
Cooking time: 35-40 minutes

1. Cook the potatoes in a pan of boiling salted water for about 25 minutes until tender. Drain and mash to a purée with the butter and salt and pepper to taste.
2. Spoon into a piping bag fitted with a star-shaped nozzle and pipe around the edges of four individual flameproof dishes or one large dish.
3. Divide the eggs between the dishes.
4. For the sauce, melt the butter in a pan. Add the flour and cook for 1 minute, stirring. Gradually add the milk to make a smooth sauce. Bring to the boil and cook for 2-3 minutes, stirring. Stir in the mustard, cheese, chives and salt and pepper to taste, blending well. Spoon over the eggs to coat.
5. Place under a preheated hot grill and cook for about 5-10 minutes until golden and bubbly. Serve at once.

Devilled Spanish pizza: Dutch cheese fondue

SPANISH-STYLE OMELETTE

50 g (2 oz) butter
1 large onion, peeled and sliced
100 g (4 oz) bacon, rinded and chopped
225 g (8 oz) cooked potato, diced
1 red pepper, cored, seeded and chopped
1 green pepper, cored, seeded and chopped
4 eggs, beaten
salt
freshly ground black pepper
1 teaspoon dried marjoram
50 g (2 oz) Cheddar cheese, grated
6 pimiento-stuffed green olives, sliced
1 teaspoon paprika pepper

Preparation time: 20 minutes
Cooking time: about 15 minutes

1. Melt the butter in a large heavy-based frying pan. Add the onion and bacon and fry until crisp and lightly browned.
2. Add the potato and peppers and cook for 2 minutes. Beat the eggs with salt and pepper to taste and the marjoram. Pour into the pan and cook over a gentle heat until the mixture is almost set.
3. Sprinkle with the cheese, olives and paprika. Place under a preheated hot grill and cook for about 3 minutes until golden.
4. Serve hot, with warm crusty bread and a salad.

CAMEMBERT PUFFS WITH FRUIT CONSERVE

8 individual wedges Camembert cheese, well chilled
2 tablespoons plain flour
2 eggs, beaten
75 g (3 oz) fresh white breadcrumbs
1-2 teaspoons mixed dried herbs
oil to deep fry
To serve:
8 tablespoons gooseberry, damson or cherry conserve

Preparation time: 30 minutes
Cooking time: 3-4 minutes

1. Dust the wedges of cheese with the flour. Dip into the beaten egg and coat in the breadcrumbs mixed with the herbs.
2. Heat the oil in a pan to 190°C/375°F or until a cube of bread browns in 30 seconds. Add the coated Camembert wedges and deep fry for about 3-4 minutes until crisp and golden.
3. Drain on paper towels. Serve very hot with the cold fruit conserve.

CHEESE AND WALNUT CROQUETTES WITH WATERCRESS DIP

100 g (4 oz) walnuts, very finely chopped
75 g (3 oz) fresh wholemeal breadcrumbs
½ small onion, peeled and grated
50 g (2 oz) Edam cheese, finely grated
1 tablespoon chopped fresh parsley
salt
freshly ground black pepper
1 egg (sizes 1, 2), beaten
1-2 tablespoons milk
2 tablespoons oil
Dip:
1 bunch watercress, very finely chopped
150 ml (¼ pint) soured cream
1 teaspoon dried mixed herbs
pinch of grated nutmeg

Preparation time: 30 minutes
Cooking time: 10 minutes

1. Mix the walnuts with the breadcrumbs, onion, cheese, parsley and salt and pepper to taste. Bind together with the egg and milk. Divide into twelve equal portions and roll each into a ball.
2. Heat the oil in a large frying pan. Add the croquettes and fry for about 10 minutes over a moderate heat until browned on all sides. Drain on paper towels.
3. Meanwhile for the dip, blend the watercress with the soured cream, herbs, nutmeg and salt and pepper to taste. Spoon into a small serving bowl.
4. Serve the croquettes with the dip while still warm.

PICKLED HERRING SALAD

1 × 340 ml (12 fl oz) jar pickled herrings, drained
3 pickled dill cucumbers, thinly sliced
2 red dessert apples, cored and sliced
1 bunch spring onions, trimmed and chopped
150 ml (¼ pint) soured cream
½ teaspoon dried dill

Preparation time: 20 minutes

1. Cut the herrings into thin strips and place in a bowl.
2. Add the sliced dill cucumbers, apples, spring onions, soured cream and dill, toss well to mix.
3. Spoon into a chilled serving dish and serve with warm crusty bread.

Spanish-style omelette; Pickled herring salad; Camembert puffs with fruit conserve

FRANKFURTER, PINEAPPLE AND PEPPER BROCHETTES

3 × 170 g (6 oz) packets Continental frankfurters
1 × 312 g (11 oz) can pineapple cubes in natural juice
2 green peppers, cored, seeded and cut into
  bite-sized pieces
1 tablespoon soy sauce
1 teaspoon oil
25 g (1 oz) stem ginger, very finely chopped
salt
freshly ground black pepper
1 teaspoon cornflour

Preparation time: 10 minutes
Cooking time: 8-10 minutes

1. Score diagonally along one side of the frankfurters, then cut into bite-sized pieces.
2. Drain the pineapple cubes, reserving the juice.
3. Thread the frankfurters on to four skewers alternating with the pineapple cubes and pepper pieces.
4. Mix the pineapple juice with the soy sauce, oil, stem ginger and salt and pepper to taste, blending well. Brush the brochettes with a little of this sauce.
5. Place under a preheated hot grill and cook until hot and bubbly, basting from time to time with the sauce.
6. Dissolve the cornflour in a little water and stir into the remaining sauce in a pan. Bring to the boil, stirring constantly until thickened.
7. Serve the cooked brochettes with the hot sauce. Accompany with plain or turmeric-flavoured rice or cooked noodles.

Frankfurter, pineapple and pepper brochettes; Cottage cheese pancakes with spreads served separately; Stuffed onions

COTTAGE CHEESE PANCAKES

Pancakes:
40 g (1½ oz) plain flour
½ teaspoon salt
175 g (6 oz) cottage cheese
25 g (1 oz) butter, melted
3 eggs, separated
2 tablespoons oil
Spreads:
150 ml (¼ pint) taramasalata
2 tablespoons snipped fresh chives
1 × 120 g (4 oz) can sardines in oil, drained
50 g (2 oz) full fat soft cheese
1 tablespoon lemon juice
3 tablespoons soured cream

Preparation time: 30 minutes
Cooking time: 8-12 minutes

1. Sift the flour and salt into a bowl. Add the cottage cheese, butter and egg yolks, blending well.
2. Whisk the egg whites until in stiff peaks and fold into the cottage cheese mixture with a metal spoon.
3. Heat half the oil in a large heavy-based frying pan and drop about 6 tablespoons of the batter into the pan, spacing well apart. Fry over a moderate heat for 2-3 minutes. Turn over with a fish slice or palette knife and cook for a further 2-3 minutes. Remove and keep warm. Repeat with the remaining oil and batter.
4. Meanwhile, spoon the taramasalata into a small bowl and sprinkle with half of the chives.
5. Place the sardines, soft cheese, lemon juice and soured cream into a blender and purée until smooth. Alternatively, mash the ingredients together with a fork until smooth. Spoon into a small bowl and sprinkle with the remaining chives.
6. Serve the pancakes warm with the fish spreads.

STUFFED ONIONS

4 large Spanish onions, peeled
salt
225 g (8 oz) lean minced beef
2 garlic cloves, peeled and crushed
50 g (2 oz) pine kernels
1 teaspoon dried mixed herbs
freshly ground black pepper
50 g (2 oz) fresh wholemeal breadcrumbs
75 g (3 oz) Cheshire cheese, grated
1 egg, beaten
150 ml (¼ pint) plain unsweetened yogurt

Preparation time: 30 minutes
Cooking time: 1 hour 20 minutes
Oven: 190°C, 375°F, Gas Mark 5

1. Boil the onions in a pan of lightly salted boiling water for 10 minutes. Drain, reserving about 150 ml (¼ pint) of the cooking liquor.
2. Scoop out the centres of the onions with a small knife or spoon and use for another dish.
3. Meanwhile, fry the beef in its own fat in a pan until lightly browned. Add the garlic, pine kernels, herbs and salt and pepper to taste. Cook for a further 5 minutes. Remove from the heat, stir in the breadcrumbs, cheese and egg, blending well.
4. Fill the onions with this mixture and place in an ovenproof dish.
5. Pour the reserved onion liquor around the stuffed onions. Place in a preheated oven and cook, covered, for 30 minutes.
6. Uncover and cook for a further 30 minutes. Serve hot, each topped with a spoonful of the yogurt.

CLOCKWISE FROM THE TOP: Crafty fish scallops: Seafood pancakes; Fish and egg envelopes

CRAFTY FISH SCALLOPS

450 g (1 lb) potatoes, peeled
25 g (1 oz) butter
salt
freshly ground black pepper
100 g (4 oz) Cheddar cheese, grated
4 × 100 g (4 oz) packets frozen cod in butter or
    parsley or mushroom sauce
To garnish:
lemon quarters
sprigs of parsley

Preparation time: 30 minutes
Cooking times: 30-35 minutes

1. Cook the potatoes in a pan of boiling salted water for about 25 minutes until tender. Drain and mash to a purée with the butter and salt and pepper to taste. Blend in half of the cheese, mixing well.
2. Meanwhile, cook the cod in sauce according to the packet instructions. Remove from the packets and flake the fish into the sauce.
3. Spoon into a piping bag fitted with a star shaped nozzle and pipe swirls of potato around the edges of four greased scallop shells. Spoon the sauce mixture into the prepared scallop shells and sprinkle with the remaining cheese.
4. Place under a preheated hot grill and cook for about 5-10 minutes until golden and bubbly.
5. Garnish with lemon and parsley.

FISH AND EGG ENVELOPES

1×400 g (14 oz) packet frozen puff pastry, thawed
350 g (12 oz) frozen white fish fillets (eg. plaice, sole,
    haddock) thawed, skinned and cut into four equal pieces
2 hard-boiled eggs, shelled and sliced
1×213 g (7½ oz) can creamed mushrooms
1 teaspoon lemon juice
4 teaspoons chopped capers
1 tablespoon snipped fresh chives
salt
freshly ground white pepper
beaten egg to glaze

Preparation time: 30 minutes
Cooking time: 20-25 minutes
Oven: 220°C, 425°F, Gas Mark 7

1. Roll out the pastry on a lightly floured surface and
cut into four 13 cm (5 inch) squares. Place on dampened baking sheets.
2. Place a piece of fish on each pastry square and top
with an equal quantity of the egg. Mix the mushrooms
with the lemon juice, capers, chives and salt and
pepper to taste. Spoon equally over the egg.
3. Brush the pastry edges with beaten egg. Bring the
corners of each pastry square together and seal to
make envelope shapes. Make a small hole in each
envelope to allow any steam to escape during
cooking. Brush with beaten egg to glaze and decorate
with any pastry trimmings.
4. Place in a preheated oven and cook for 20-25
minutes until well risen, golden brown and cooked
through. Serve hot with salad or stuffed baked
tomatoes.

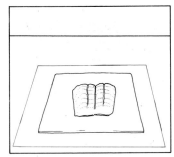
Put a piece of fish on the pastry.

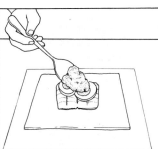
Spoon over the egg and mushroom mixture.

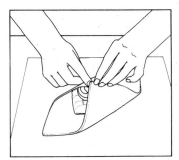
Bring the corners together to seal.

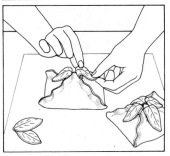
Glaze and add pastry trimmings.

SEAFOOD PANCAKES

Pancake batter:
100 g (4 oz) plain flour
1 egg
300 ml (½ pint) milk
1 tablespoon oil
pinch of salt
Filling:
25 g (1 oz) butter
25 g (1 oz) plain flour
4 tablespoons dry white wine
150 ml (¼ pint) fish or chicken stock
½ tablespoon tomato purée
salt
freshly ground black pepper
4 tablespoons double cream or creamy milk
1 tablespoon chopped fresh parsley
175 g (6 oz) canned prawns or shrimps
1×150 g (5 oz) can mussels in brine, drained and chopped
2×40 g (1½ oz) cans crabmeat, drained and flaked
1 teaspoon lemon juice

Preparation time: 20 minutes
Cooking time: 50 minutes
Oven: 180°C, 350°F, Gas Mark 4

The clever trick which makes this dish so speedy
is the use of a blender to make the pancakes.

1. Place the batter ingredients in a blender goblet and
blend on maximum speed for 30 seconds.
2. Heat a large omelette pan and add a few drops of oil.
Pour in 1-2 tablespoons of the batter, tilt the pan to
coat the bottom evenly. Cook until the underside is
brown, then turn and cook for 10 seconds. Repeat
with the remaining batter, stacking the pancakes as
they are cooked. ⑤
3. For the filling, melt the butter in a pan. Add the
flour and cook for 1 minute, stirring. Gradually add
the wine and stock to make a smooth sauce. Bring to
the boil and cook for 2-3 minutes, stirring. Add the
tomato purée and salt and pepper to taste, and simmer
gently for 10 minutes. Add the cream and half the
parsley.
4. Mix the prawns, mussels and crabmeat with half
the sauce. Fill each pancake with an equal quantity of
this filling and roll up. Place in a greased ovenproof
dish.
5. Mix the remaining sauce with the lemon juice and
pour over the pancakes. Place in a preheated oven and
cook for about 10-15 minutes until heated through.
6. Sprinkle with the remaining parsley and serve.

⑤ Freeze pancakes interleaved with foil or greaseproof paper for up to 4 months. Allow to thaw in their
wrappings for about 1-2 hours at room temperature.

SALADS, PASTRIES & PÂTÉS

ITALIAN PLATTER

Dressing:
3 tablespoons red wine vinegar
1 tablespoon lemon juice
1 small garlic clove, peeled and crushed
1½ teaspoons wholegrain mustard
8 tablespoons olive or salad oil
salt
freshly ground black pepper
Platter:
4 medium new potatoes, boiled in their skins
4 tablespoons mayonnaise
1 tablespoon chopped fresh parsley
1×400 g (14 oz) can artichoke hearts, drained
1×400 g (14 oz) can flageolet or cannellini beans, drained
1×120 g (4½ oz) can sardines in oil, drained
50 g (2 oz) salami or garlic sausage, rinded and rolled into cornets
2 hard-boiled eggs, shelled and quartered
8 cherry tomatoes
1×50 g (2 oz) can anchovy fillets in oil, drained

Preparation time: 30 minutes

1. For the dressing, in a bowl beat the vinegar with the lemon juice, garlic and mustard. Gradually add the oil to make a thickened dressing. Add salt and pepper to taste. Ⓐ
2. Slice the potatoes and mix with the mayonnaise, parsley and salt and pepper to taste.
3. Arrange the artichoke hearts, beans, sardines, salami or garlic sausage, eggs and potato salad around the edge of a large platter like the spokes of a wheel.
4. Cut a cross in the top of each tomato and open out slightly. Place the tomatoes in the centre of the platter and cover with a lattice of anchovy.
5. Drizzle the dressing over the whole of the platter and serve with crusty bread.

Ⓐ The dressing can be made in a screw-topped jar and stored in the refrigerator for up to 3 weeks. Shake vigorously to mix before using.

PAPAYA PRAWNS

4 large papayas, about 225 g (8 oz) each
2 teaspoons fresh lime juice
8 large king prawns, peeled and chopped
1 red pepper, cored, seeded and chopped
120 ml (4 fl oz) mayonnaise
2 teaspoons freshly grated horseradish
finely grated rind of 1 lime
To garnish:
twists of lime
few whole unpeeled prawns (optional)

Preparation time: 20 minutes

With pink-orange flesh, similar to that of a melon, papayas are sometimes called pawpaws. By serving one shell per person, you can also make an unusual starter for 8.

1. Slice the papayas in half lengthways, scoop out and discard the seeds. Carefully scoop out the flesh with a melon baller or cut into small cubes, leaving the shells intact.
2. Mix the papaya flesh with the lime juice, prawns, red pepper, mayonnaise, horseradish and grated lime rind, blending well.
3. Spoon the papaya and prawn mixture back into the reserved shells. Place two shells on each of four individual serving plates.
4. Chill lightly before serving garnished with twists of lime and a few unpeeled prawns (if used). Serve with triangles of brown bread and butter.

A papaya resembles an elongated melon and its ripeness and preparation for eating is very similar. A papaya is ripe when the skin turns yellow and feels tender when lightly presed, especially at the stalk end.

To prepare, halve lengthways and scoop out the seeds with a metal spoon, removing any attached seed membrane from the pink papaya flesh. The flesh can then be scooped from each papaya half with a melon baller or teaspoon.

Papaya prawns; Italian platter

CUCUMBER, MELON AND HAM SALAD

1 Ogen or small honeydew melon
1 slice cooked ham, about 225 g (8 oz)
4 tomatoes, quartered
75 g (3 oz) black grapes, halved and seeded
¼ cucumber, very thinly sliced
Dressing:
4 tablespoons soured cream
2 tablespoons chopped spring onions
1 teaspoon chopped fresh mint
salt
freshly ground black pepper
To garnish:
few sprigs fresh mint

Preparation time: 25 minutes

1. Slice the melon in half, scoop out the seeds and discard. Remove the flesh with a melon baller or cut into bite-sized cubes. Reserve the melon shells for serving if wished.
2. Cut the ham into thin julienne strips. Place in a bowl with the melon, tomatoes, grapes and cucumber, tossing gently to mix.
3. Mix the soured cream with the spring onion, mint and salt and pepper to taste. Ⓐ
4. Mix the salad ingredients with the dressing, tossing gently to mix. Spoon into a serving bowl or return to the melon shells to serve.
5. Garnish with a few sprigs of mint before serving.

Ⓐ The dressing can be made in advance and stored in the refrigerator for up to 3 days. Stir well to blend before using.

FROM THE LEFT: Cucumber, melon and ham salad; Midsummer chicken; Smoked trout and orange salad

SMOKED TROUT AND ORANGE SALAD

350 g (12 oz) smoked trout fillets, skinned and boned
½ cucumber, very thinly sliced
3 oranges, peeled, pith removed and segmented
3 sticks celery, trimmed, scrubbed and thinly sliced
Dressing:
40 g (1½ oz) sweet apple, grated
1 tablespoon lemon juice
3 tablespoons mayonnaise
1½ teaspoons creamed horseradish
To garnish:
few lettuce leaves
1 bunch watercress
cayenne pepper

Preparation time: 20 minutes

1. To make the dressing, mix the apple with the lemon juice, mayonnaise and creamed horseradish, blending well. Ⓐ
2. Flake the smoked trout into bite-sized pieces. Place in a serving bowl with the cucumber, orange segments and celery, tossing gently to mix.
3. To serve, line a serving dish with a few lettuce leaves. Top with the smoked trout salad and spoon over the dressing.
4. Chill lightly before serving garnished with sprigs of watercress and sprinkled with cayenne pepper.

Ⓐ The dressing can be stored in the refrigerator for up to 3 days. Stir well to blend before using.

MIDSUMMER CHICKEN

450 g (1 lb) cooked chicken meat, skinned and boned
100 ml (3½ fl oz) dry white wine
1 teaspoon lemon juice
2 teaspoons grated onion
1 teaspoon chopped fresh tarragon
pinch of onion salt
4 oranges, peeled, pith removed and segmented
100 g (4 oz) lamb's lettuce, endive, or small lettuce leaves, rinsed
1 bunch watercress, rinsed
50 g (2 oz) toasted pine nuts or walnuts
Dressing:
75 g (3 oz) full fat soft cheese
150 ml (¼ pint) soured cream
3 drops Tabasco sauce
salt
freshly ground black pepper
To garnish:
julienne strips of orange rind

Preparation time: 30 minutes, plus marinating

1. Slice the chicken into thin strips. Place in a bowl with the wine, lemon juice, onion, tarragon, onion salt and orange segments, blending well. Cover and leave to marinate for 20 minutes.
2. Meanwhile, toss the lettuce or endive with the watercress and use to line a serving plate.
3. Remove the chicken and orange segments from the marinade and mix with the pine nuts or walnuts, reserving the marinade. Spoon the chicken mixture on to the lettuce or endive and watercress.
4. Blend the cheese with the soured cream, Tabasco and salt and pepper to taste. Add sufficient marinade, about 1-2 tablespoons, to give the dressing a thick pouring consistency. Pour over the chicken mixture.
5. Briefly blanch a few julienne strips of orange rind. Sprinkle over the lightly chilled chicken mixture.

SPICY MEXICAN SALAD

1 × 312 g (11 oz) can sweetcorn kernels, drained
1 × 425 g (15 oz) can red kidney beans, drained
1 small onion, peeled and thinly sliced into rings
1 small green pepper, cored, seeded and thinly sliced
175 g (6 oz) chorizo sausage, skinned and sliced
    or salami, chopped
Dressing:
4 tablespoons mayonnaise
2 tablespoons chilli relish
½ teaspoon mild chilli powder
1 tablespoon finely chopped red pepper
pinch of salt

Preparation time: 20 minutes

Use this spicy dressing in salads, sandwiches and also as a delicious topping for jacket baked potatoes.

1. In a large salad bowl, mix the sweetcorn kernels with the kidney beans, onion rings, green pepper and chorizo sausage or salami, tossing gently to mix.
2. Mix the mayonnaise with the chilli relish, chilli powder, red pepper and salt, blending well. Ⓐ
3. Just before serving, spoon the dressing over the salad ingredients and toss well to mix.
4. Chill lightly before serving. Serve with tortillas, corn chips or crisp crackers.

Ⓐ The dressing can be made in advance and stored in the refrigerator for up to 3 days. Stir before using.

TROPICAL CURRIED CHICKEN SALAD

350 g (12 oz) cooked chicken meat, skinned and boned
2 bananas, peeled and sliced
1 tablespoon lemon juice
50 g (2 oz) cashew nuts (salted or unsalted)
25 g (1 oz) raisins
50 g (2 oz) dried apricots, coarsely chopped
Dressing:
3 tablespoons mayonnaise
1 tablespoon finely chopped onion
½ teaspoon hot Madras curry powder
½ teaspoon lemon juice
2 tablespoons grated sweet apple
1 teaspoon mango chutney
pinch of salt
To garnish:
1 tablespoon long-thread coconut, toasted

Preparation time: 20 minutes

For special occasions, serve this salad on bought plain or spiced poppadums.

1. To make the dressing, mix the mayonnaise with the onion, curry powder, lemon juice, apple, chutney and salt, blending well. Ⓐ
2. Cut the chicken into bite-sized pieces. Place in a serving bowl with the bananas and lemon juice, tossing gently to mix. Add the cashew nuts, raisins and dried apricots, blending well.
3. Just before serving, spoon the dressing over the salad ingredients and toss well to mix.
4. Chill lightly before serving sprinkled with the toasted coconut.

Ⓐ The dressing can be stored in the refrigerator, tightly covered, for up to 3 days. Stir before using.

SEAFOOD PASTA

175 g (6 oz) pasta twists
1 avocado, peeled, stoned and sliced
2 teaspoons lemon juice
175 g (6 oz) peeled prawns
1 × 200 g (7 oz) jar mussels in brine, rinsed and drained
3 tomatoes, cut into wedges
50 g (2 oz) button mushrooms, sliced
Dressing:
2 tablespoons mayonnaise
2 tablespoons soured cream
¾-1 teaspoon garlic purée
2 teaspoons snipped chives
salt
freshly ground black pepper
To garnish:
few whole unpeeled prawns

Preparation time: 30 minutes
Cooking time: about 10 minutes

1. Cook the pasta twists in boiling salted water according to the packet instructions, for about 8-10 minutes. Drain and allow to cool.
2. In a bowl, toss the avocado slices in the lemon juice and add the pasta with the prawns, mussels, tomatoes and mushrooms, mixing gently.
3. Mix the mayonnaise with the soured cream, garlic purée, chives and salt and pepper to taste.
4. Fold the dressing into the salad and spoon into a serving dish. Chill lightly then garnish with prawns.

Ⓐ The dressing can be stored tightly covered in the refrigerator for up to 3 days. Stir well before using.

TOP TO BOTTOM: Seafood pasta; Tropical curried chicken salad

CHICKEN AND HAM LOAF

Serves 6-8
1 crusty sandwich loaf
75 g (3 oz) butter
2 small onions, peeled and finely chopped
225 g (8 oz) mushrooms, thinly sliced
1 tablespoon chopped fresh parsley
salt
freshly ground black pepper
225 g (8 oz) sausage meat
175 g (6 oz) lean bacon, rinded and chopped
225 g (8 oz) cooked ham, chopped
2 tablespoons dry sherry (optional)
¼ teaspoon dried sage
¼ teaspoon dried thyme
225 g (8 oz) cooked chicken meat, skinned, boned
   and chopped
To garnish:
sprigs of Continental parsley

Preparation time: 30 minutes
Cooking time: 1¼-1½ hours
Oven: 190°C, 375°F, Gas Mark 5

1. Cut a 1 cm (½ inch) slice lengthways off the top of the loaf and carefully pull out the soft bread inside. Leave a 1 cm (½ inch) inner lining of bread to keep the shape. Use the inner bread to make breadcrumbs.
2. Melt 50 g (2 oz) of the butter and use to brush the loaf, inside and out. Replace the lid and brush with any remaining melted butter. Put on a baking sheet, place in a preheated oven and cook for 10 minutes or until crisp and golden.
3. Meanwhile, melt the remaining butter in a pan. Add the onions and fry for 5 minutes until soft. Add the mushrooms and cook for a further 2 minutes. Stir in the parsley and salt and pepper to taste. Remove from the heat.
4. Mix the sausage meat with the bacon, ham and 3 tablespoons of the breadcrumbs. Stir in the sherry, if used, sage and thyme, blending well.
5. Press half of the sausage meat mixture into the bread case. Cover with half of the onion mixture. Arrange the chicken on top and cover with the remaining onion and sausage meat mixtures. Replace the lid and wrap the loaf in foil.
6. Return to the oven and bake for 1 hour. Serve the loaf, hot or cold, cut into thick slices with salad and garnished with parsley.

PEAR WALDORF SALAD

1 lettuce, washed and shredded
2 sticks celery, trimmed, scrubbed and chopped
1 red pepper, cored, seeded and sliced
25 g (1 oz) walnut halves
75 g (3 oz) green grapes, peeled, halved and seeded
1 dessert pear, peeled, cored and sliced
225 g (8 oz) smoked chicken, skinned and boned
Dressing:
2 tablespoons plain unsweetened yogurt
2 tablespoons mayonnaise
2 tablespoons grated cucumber
1 teaspoon grated onion
½ teaspoon chopped fresh tarragon
salt
freshly ground black pepper
To garnish:
1 dessert pear, cored and sliced
few sprigs fresh tarragon

Preparation time: 25 minutes

A variation of the classic Waldorf salad, so called because it was invented by the chef of the Waldorf hotel New York, Pear waldorf salad combines pears with the classic ingredients and a tasty cucumber and tarragon dressing.

1. In a large salad bowl, mix the lettuce with the celery, red pepper, walnuts, grapes, pear and smoked chicken.
2. Mix the yogurt with the mayonnaise, cucumber, onion and tarragon, blending well. Add salt and pepper to taste. Ⓐ
3. Just before serving, spoon the dressing over the salad ingredients and toss well to mix.
4. Garnish with slices of pear and a few sprigs of fresh tarragon.

Ⓐ The dressing can be made in advance and stored in the refrigerator for up to 3 days. Stir well to blend before using.

Variation:
Pear Waldorf salad can also be made using a soured cream dressing made by mixing 2 tablespoons soured cream with 2 tablespoons mayonnaise, 1 tablespoon grated courgette or cucumber, 2 teaspoons grated onion, 1 tablespoon chopped roast peanuts and salt and pepper to taste.

Chicken and ham loaf; Pear Waldorf salad

SMOKED MACKEREL MOUSSE

Serves 4-6
350 g (12 oz) smoked mackerel, skinned and boned
1½ tablespoons lemon juice
135 ml (4½ fl oz) lemon mayonnaise
1 tablespoon creamed horseradish
salt
freshly ground black pepper
4 teaspoons powdered gelatine
4 tablespoons water
120 ml (4 fl oz) double cream
To garnish:
lemon slices
few sprigs watercress

Preparation time: 20 minutes, plus chilling
Cooking time: 5 minutes

1. Mash the mackerel with the lemon juice, mayonnaise, creamed horseradish and salt and pepper to taste. Alternatively, purée until smooth in a blender.
2. Sprinkle the gelatine over the water in a small bowl. Leave for 5 minutes to soften. Place in a small pan of hot water and heat until completely dissolved. Fold into the mackerel mixture.
3. Whip the cream until it stands in soft peaks. Fold into the mackerel mixture with a metal spoon. Spoon into an oiled 900 ml (1½ pint) ring or fish-shaped mould and chill for about 2 hours until set. Ⓐ Ⓕ
4. To serve, dip the mould briefly into hot water and invert on to a serving dish.
5. Garnish with lemon slices and a few watercress sprigs before serving. Serve with crisp Melba toast or fingers of warm wholemeal toast.

Ⓐ Smoked mackerel mousse can be made in advance and stored in the refrigerator for up to 3 days.
Ⓕ Wrap the mould in cling film and overwrap in a freezer bag. Freeze for up to 1 month. To thaw, unwrap and thaw overnight in the refrigerator or for 4-5 hours at room temperature.

CREAMY MACKEREL PÂTÉ EN CROÛTE

Serves 6
175 g (6 oz) plain flour
pinch of salt
40 g (1½ oz) butter
40 g (1½ oz) lard
finely grated rind of ½ lemon
2 tablespoons iced water
Filling:
50 g (2 oz) butter
350 g (12 oz) smoked mackerel, skinned, boned and flaked
2 tablespoons lemon juice
175 g (6 oz) full fat soft cheese
1 egg, beaten
¼ teaspoon freshly ground black pepper
2 canned pimientos, chopped
50 g (2 oz) capers, coarsely chopped
3 tablespoons chopped fresh parsley
beaten egg to glaze

Preparation time: 30 minutes
Cooking time: 45 minutes
Oven: 200°C, 400°F, Gas Mark 6

A spring onion curl makes a special garnish for this dish (see page 58).

1. Sift the flour and salt into a mixing bowl. Rub the butter and lard into the flour with the fingertips until the mixture resembles fine breadcrumbs. Stir in the lemon rind, blending well. Add the water and bind to a firm but pliable dough. Turn on to a lightly floured surface and knead until smooth.
2. Roll out three-quarters of the prepared pastry to a rectangle large enough to line a greased 750 ml (1¼ pint) oblong foil loaf dish or small loaf tin.
3. For the filling, melt the butter in a pan. Add the flaked mackerel and cook gently for 2-3 minutes. Remove from the heat and add the lemon juice, cheese, egg and pepper, mixing well to blend. Allow to cool slightly.
4. Layer the pimiento on the base of the pastry in the loaf tin and top with the capers. Cover with half of the mackerel mixture. Cover with a layer of parsley and top with the remaining mackerel mixture.
5. Roll out the remaining pastry to make a lid. Dampen the pastry rim with water and cover with the lid. Trim, seal and flute the edges. Use any pastry trimmings to make leaves to decorate the lid. Brush with beaten egg to glaze.
6. Place in a preheated oven and cook for about 40 minutes. Cool then chill before turning out of the tin and slicing to serve. Serve with a crisp salad.

CHEESE AND ONION RING

Serves 4-6
175 g (6 oz) Double Gloucester cheese, grated
½ teaspoon dried mixed herbs
2 onions, peeled and finely chopped
2 tablespoons mild mustard pickle
salt
freshly ground black pepper
1 × 398 g (13 oz) packet frozen shortcrust pastry, thawed
beaten egg, to glaze
poppy seeds or cracked wheat to sprinkle
To garnish:
endive or 2 bunches watercress

Preparation time: 30 minutes
Cooking time: 30-35 minutes
Oven: 200°C, 400°F, Gas Mark 6

Creamy mackerel pâté en croûte; Cheese and onion ring

1. In a bowl, mix the cheese with the herbs, onion, mustard pickle and salt and pepper to taste, blending together well.

2. Roll out the pastry on a lightly floured surface to a rectangle measuring 40×28 cm (16×11 inches).

3. Spread the cheese filling over the pastry with a spatula to within 1 cm (½ inch) of the edges. Brush one long edge with beaten egg to glaze. Roll up from the opposite long edge, like a Swiss roll. Press firmly along the glazed edge to seal. Place seam-side down on a greased baking sheet.

4. Using scissors, snip across the long edge of the roll at 2.5 cm (1 inch) intervals, almost through to the other edge. Shape the roll into a ring, brush the ends with beaten egg to glaze and press together to seal firmly.

5. Carefully lift each cut section of the ring and tilt slightly sideways so that the filling is just exposed. Brush the ring with beaten egg and sprinkle with poppy seeds or cracked wheat.

6. Place in a preheated oven and cook for 30-35 minutes or until golden brown and cooked through. Allow to cool slightly on a wire tray. Serve the ring warm garnished with endive or watercress.

Brush one long edge with egg.

Roll up and place seam-side down.

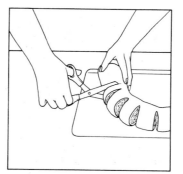

Snip pastry at intervals while shaping into ring.

Tilt edges and brush with egg.

CIDERED FARMHOUSE PÂTÉ

Serves 8

6 rashers streaky bacon, rinded
75 g (3 oz) butter
225 g (8 oz) pig's liver, chopped
225 g (8 oz) fat bacon, chopped
1 large onion, peeled and chopped
1 garlic clove, peeled and crushed
25 g (1 oz) plain flour
150 ml (¼ pint) milk
150 ml (¼ pint) dry cider
salt
freshly ground black pepper
4 bay leaves
6 allspice berries
5 tablespoons liquid aspic (optional)

Preparation time: 30 minutes
Cooking time: 1¼ hours
Oven: 180°C, 350°F, Gas Mark 4

1. Lay the streaky bacon on a board and stretch with the back of a knife. Use to line the base and sides of a greased 450 g (1 lb) terrine.
2. Melt 50 g (2 oz) of the butter in a large pan. Add the liver, fat bacon, onion and garlic and cook for 10 minutes. Mince or purée until smooth in a blender.
3. Melt the remaining butter in a pan. Add the flour and cook for 1 minute. Gradually add the milk and cider, blending well. Bring to the boil, stirring constantly, and cook for 2-3 minutes. Add plenty of salt and pepper to taste. Stir into the liver mixture. Spoon into the terrine, levelling the surface.
4. Top with the bay leaves and allspice berries. Cover with buttered foil or a lid and place in a roasting tin half-full of hot water. Place in a preheated oven and cook for about 1 hour or until just firm to the touch. Allow to cool then chill lightly. Ⓐ Ⓕ
5. If the pâté is to be eaten over 2 days, a thin layer of aspic poured over the surface will keep it moist.

Ⓐ Store in the refrigerator for up to 1 week.
Ⓕ To freeze, wrap the terrine in cling film then over-wrap in a freezer bag. Freeze for up to 2 months. To thaw, remove the wrappings and leave overnight in the refrigerator or for 4-5 hours at room temperature.

STUFFED FRENCH BREAD

Serves 3
1 large long crusty French stick
25 g (1 oz) butter
Coleslaw:
100 g (4 oz) white cabbage, grated
25 g (1 oz) onion, grated
1 small carrot, peeled and grated
1 stick celery, scrubbed and chopped
15 g (½ oz) raisins
3 walnuts, coarsely chopped
3-4 tablespoons mayonnaise
Filling:
2 lettuce leaves, washed and shredded
3 slices Mortadella, rinded and rolled
25 g (1 oz) salami, rinded and rolled into cornets
50 g (2 oz) smoked cheese, rinded and sliced
50 g (2 oz) blue cheese, sliced
1 hard-boiled egg, shelled and sliced
1 large beef tomato, sliced

Preparation time: 25 minutes

1. To make the coleslaw, mix the cabbage with the onion, carrot, celery, raisins and walnuts, mixing well. Bind together with the mayonnaise. Ⓐ
2. Split the loaf in half horizontally. Butter the inside of the loaf thinly.
3. Spread the coleslaw along the length of the bottom half of the loaf and top with the lettuce, Mortadella, salami, smoked cheese, blue cheese, egg and tomato, arranging attractively.
4. Press the loaf halves firmly together and cut vertically into 3 thick sections to serve.

Ⓐ The coleslaw can be made in advance and stored in the refrigerator for up to 5 days.

Variation:
For an Oriental flavour substitute the white cabbage by shredded Chinese leaves, the celery by beansprouts and the onion by waterchestnuts in the coleslaw. Use on same day.

MUSHROOM CREAM QUICHE

Serves 4-6
225 g (8 oz) plain flour
¼ teaspoon salt
100 g (4 oz) butter, cut into small pieces
2 tablespoons iced water
Filling:
25 g (1 oz) butter
1 small onion, peeled and chopped
225 g (8 oz) small button mushrooms
150 ml (¼ pint) plain unsweetened yogurt
150 ml (¼ pint) double cream
3 eggs, beaten
2 teaspoons mixed dried herbs
2 teaspoons snipped chives or chopped spring onion tops
salt
freshly ground black pepper

Preparation time: 25 minutes
Cooking time: 50 minutes
Oven: 200°C, 400°F, Gas Mark 6;
then: 180°C, 350°F, Gas Mark 4

By the use of shortcrust made in a blender this quiche becomes superbly quick, and easy. If you wish to make the pastry without the aid of a blender, simply rub the fat into the flour in the usual way and bind together with the iced water.

1. Place the flour, salt and butter in a blender goblet or bowl. Mix on the lowest speed, increasing to medium speed, until the mixture resembles fine breadcrumbs, about ½-1 minute. Add the water and mix on the lowest speed until the ingredients just bind together. Turn on to a lightly floured surface and knead lightly until smooth and free from cracks. Ⓐ
2. Roll out to a round large enough to line a lightly greased 21-23 cm (8½-9 inch) flan dish or ring set on a lightly greased baking sheet. Ⓕ
3. Line the flan with greaseproof paper, then fill with baking beans. Place in a preheated oven and bake blind for 15 minutes.
4. Meanwhile for the filling, melt the butter in a pan. Add the onion and cook for about 5 minutes until softened. Add the mushrooms and cook for 2-3 minutes. Remove from the heat.
5. Mix the yogurt with the cream and eggs. Add to the mushroom mixture, blending well. Add the dried herbs, chives or onion and salt and pepper to taste.
6. Remove the greaseproof paper with the beans. Spoon the mushroom mixture into the flan case. Reduce the oven temperature and bake for a further 35 minutes until set. Serve hot or cold, cut into wedges.

Ⓐ The shortcrust pastry can be made in advance, wrapped in foil and stored in the refrigerator for up to 1 week.
Ⓕ Open freeze the uncooked flan case in its dish or ring then wrap in foil or a freezer bag. Freeze for up to 3 months. Cook from frozen, increasing the initial blind baking by 5-10 minutes.

Stuffed French bread; Cidered farmhouse pâté

Ham and smoked cheese flan; Spanish quiche

HAM AND SMOKED CHEESE FLAN

Serves 4-6
175 g (6 oz) wholemeal flour
¼ teaspoon salt
40 g (1½ oz) butter
40 g (1½ oz) lard
2 tablespoons iced water
Filling:
175 g (6 oz) cooked ham, chopped
100 g (4 oz) smoked cheese, finely chopped
3 eggs, beaten
150 ml (¼ pint) single cream
pinch of salt
¼ teaspoon ground nutmeg
To garnish:
3 tomatoes, sliced

Preparation time: 30 minutes
Cooking time: 50 minutes
Oven: 200°C, 400°F, Gas Mark 6;
then: 180°C, 350°F, Gas Mark 4

1. Mix the wholemeal flour with the salt in a bowl. Rub in the butter and lard with the fingertips until the mixture resembles fine breadcrumbs. Add the water and bind together to a firm but pliable dough. Turn on to a lightly floured surface and knead until smooth and free from cracks. Ⓐ
2. Roll out the pastry to a round large enough to line a greased 20 cm (8 inch) flan tin. Ⓕ
3. Prick the base well with a fork. Line the flan with greaseproof paper, then fill with baking beans, dried peas or lentils. Place in a preheated oven and bake blind for 15 minutes.
4. Remove the greaseproof paper with the beans, peas or lentils from the flan. Sprinkle the ham and cheese over the base of the flan. Mix the eggs with the cream, salt and nutmeg and spoon over the ham and cheese filling. Reduce the oven temperature and bake for a further 35 minutes until set.
5. Serve the flan warm or cold, garnished with slices of tomato.

Ⓐ The wholemeal shortcrust pastry can be stored in the refrigerator for up to 1 week.
Ⓕ Open freeze the uncooked flan case then wrap in foil or a freezer bag. Freeze for up to 3 months. Cook from frozen, increasing the initial blind baking by 5-10 minutes.

SPANISH QUICHE

Serves 4-6
75 g (3 oz) full fat soft cheese
75 g (3 oz) butter
1 tablespoon single cream
¼ teaspoon salt
200 g (7 oz) plain flour
25 g (1 oz) cornflour
Filling:
25 g (1 oz) butter
1 small red pepper, cored, seeded and sliced
1 small green pepper, cored, seeded and sliced
50 g (2 oz) mushrooms, sliced
1 small courgette, very thinly sliced
75 g (3 oz) cooked ham, chopped
2 eggs, beaten
150 ml (¼ pint) double cream
1 tablespoon grated Parmesan cheese
salt
freshly ground black pepper

Preparation time: 30 minutes
Cooking time: 55 minutes
Oven: 200°C, 400°F, Gas Mark 6;
then: 180°C, 350°F, Gas Mark 4

1. Cream the cheese with the butter, single cream and salt until light and fluffy. Sift the flour with the cornflour and add to the creamed mixture. Mix to a fairly soft dough with a round-bladed knife. Turn on to a lightly floured surface and knead lightly until smooth and free from cracks. Wrap in cling film and chill for 15 minutes. Ⓐ
2. Meanwhile for the filling, melt the butter in a pan. Add the peppers, mushrooms and courgette and cook gently for 5 minutes. Remove from the heat.
3. Roll out the pastry on a lightly floured surface and line a greased 20 cm (8 inch) flan tin or dish. Ⓕ
4. Line the flan with greaseproof paper, then fill with baking beans. Place in a preheated oven and bake blind for 15 minutes.
5. Remove the greaseproof paper with the beans. Sprinkle the ham over the base of the pastry and top with the pepper mixture. Beat the eggs with the cream, Parmesan cheese and salt and pepper to taste. Spoon over the ham and pepper mixture.
6. Reduce the oven temperature and bake for a further 35 minutes until set. Serve warm or cold.

Ⓐ The cheese pastry can be stored in the refrigerator for up to 1 week.
Ⓕ Open freeze the uncooked flan case in its tin or dish then wrap in foil or a freezer bag. Freeze for up to 2 months. Cook from frozen, increasing the initial blind baking by 5-10 minutes.

ONION AND SMOKED PORK FLAN

Serves 4-6
8 oz (225 g) shortcrust pastry (see Mushroom Cream
  Quiche, page 45)
Filling:
75 g (3 oz) butter
450 g (1 lb) onions, peeled and thinly sliced
100 g (4 oz) smoked pork, chopped
25 g (1 oz) plain flour
300 ml (½ pint) milk
1 egg yolk, beaten
1 tablespoon double cream
½ teaspoon ground nutmeg
salt
freshly ground black pepper

Preparation time: 20 minutes
Cooking time: 35-40 minutes
Oven: 220°C, 425°F, Gas Mark 7

1. Roll out the prepared pastry on a lightly floured surface to a round large enough to line a greased 23 cm (9 inch) flan tin. Ⓐ Ⓕ
2. Prick the base of the flan, line with greaseproof paper and fill with baking beans. Place in a preheated oven and bake blind for 10 minutes.
3. Meanwhile for the filling, melt 50 g (2 oz) of the butter in a pan, add the onions and cook, over a moderate heat, until golden. Remove from the heat and mix with the pork.
4. Melt the remaining butter in a pan. Add the flour and cook for 1 minute. Gradually add the milk, blending well. Bring to the boil, stirring constantly, and cook for 2-3 minutes. Remove from the heat and stir in the egg yolk, cream, nutmeg and salt and pepper to taste.
5. Mix the onion and pork mixture with the sauce. Remove the greaseproof paper with the beans from the flan. Spoon in the onion mixture and cook for a further 20-25 minutes or until set. Ⓕ
6. Serve the flan very hot or cold.

Ⓐ The shortcrust pastry can be made in advance, wrapped in foil and stored in the refrigerator for up to 1 week.
Ⓕ Open freeze the uncooked flan case in its tin then wrap in foil or a freezer bag. Freeze for up to 3 months. Cook from frozen, increasing the initial blind baking by 5-10 minutes.
  Alternatively, open freeze the cooked flan until firm. Wrap in cling film and overwrap in a freezer bag. Freeze for up to 2 months. To thaw, unwrap and reheat from frozen at 180°C, 350°F, Gas Mark 4 for 30-40 minutes or until heated through. If serving cold, thaw at room temperature for about 4 hours.

TV & SHORT-CUT SUPPERS

MEDALLIONS OF PORK WITH ORANGE AND GINGER

25 g (1 oz) butter
450 g (1 lb) pork fillet or tenderloin, sliced into
    5 mm (¼ inch) rounds or medallions
salt
freshly ground black pepper
1 tablespoon ginger marmalade
1 tablespoon brown sugar
1 tablespoon orange juice
1 tablespoon cider vinegar
4 spring onions, trimmed and finely shredded
To garnish:
julienne strips of orange rind
sprigs of mint

Preparation time: 15 minutes
Cooking time: 10-12 minutes

Medallions of pork with orange and ginger are delicious served with baby onions in a white sauce.

1. Melt the butter in a frying pan. Add the pork and salt and pepper to taste. Brown quickly on all sides for about 6-8 minutes until golden and tender. Remove with a slotted spoon and arrange decoratively on a warmed serving plate. Keep warm.
2. Add the marmalade, sugar, orange juice, cider vinegar and spring onions to the pan juices. Heat until the mixture forms a syrupy glaze.
3. Spoon over the pork medallions and garnish with julienne strips of orange rind and mint sprigs.

Variation:
Medallions of pork can also be cooked with apricots and cinnamon. Add 1 tablespoon apricot jam and a pinch of ground cinnamon to the pan juices instead of the ginger marmalade in the above recipe. Soak 2 tablespoons finely chopped dried apricots and use these to garnish the dish instead of the julienne strips of orange rind.

ORANGE AND HONEY POUSSINS

3 tablespoons clear honey
1 tablespoon Dijon mustard
1 tablespoon oil
300 ml (½ pint) orange juice
3 tablespoons tomato purée
grated rind of 1 orange
1 teaspoon creamed horseradish
1 tablespoon lemon juice
½ teaspoon ground ginger
salt
freshly ground black pepper
4 poussins, cleaned and trussed
To garnish:
sprigs of watercress

Preparation time: 10 minutes
Cooking time: 1 hour
Oven: 190°C, 375°F, Gas Mark 5

1. Place the honey, mustard, oil, orange juice, tomato purée, orange rind, horseradish, lemon juice, ginger and salt and pepper to taste in a pan. Bring to the boil and cook over a moderate heat for about 10 minutes until syrupy.
2. Arrange the poussins in a roasting tin and brush liberally with orange and honey glaze. Place in a preheated oven and cook for 45 minutes or until cooked and golden, basting the poussins frequently with the syrup. If necessary, cover with foil during the last part of cooking.
3. Remove the poussins from the tin with a slotted spoon and place on a warmed serving dish. Add the remaining glaze to the tin and boil until reduced to a thick syrupy consistency.
4. Spoon over the poussins and serve hot, garnished with watercress sprigs.

Variation:
To ring the changes it is also possible to cook pineapple and honey poussins. Simply substitute unsweetened pineapple juice for the orange juice and the grated rind of 1 lemon for the orange rind in the above recipe.

Medallions of pork with orange and ginger; Orange and honey poussins

Pork chops with spicy mustard cream; Escalopes of veal Neufchâtel

PORK CHOPS WITH SPICY MUSTARD CREAM

1 tablespoon oil
4 pork chops, about 175 g (6 oz) each
4 tablespoons wholegrain mustard
1 teaspoon grated nutmeg
300 ml (½ pint) dry white wine or dry white wine and
    chicken stock mixed
salt
freshly ground black pepper
150 ml (¼ pint) double cream
1 tablespoon chopped fresh parsley

Preparation time: 5 minutes
Cooking time: 35-40 minutes

1. Heat the oil in a deep frying pan with a lid. Score the fat on the pork chops, add to the pan and brown quickly on both sides. Remove and keep warm.
2. Add the mustard, nutmeg, wine and salt and pepper to taste to the pan, blending well. Return the chops to the pan, cover and simmer gently for 20 minutes.
3. Add the cream and cook gently until the sauce reduces and thickens. Serve hot, sprinkled with the chopped parsley.
4. Serve with freshly cooked green noodles and a crisp salad.

ESCALOPES OF VEAL NEUFCHÂTEL

25 g (1 oz) butter
1 tablespoon oil
4 veal escalopes, about 100 g (4 oz) each
salt
freshly ground black pepper
1 onion, peeled and finely chopped
2 teaspoons plain flour
300 ml (½ pint) chicken stock
2 tablespoons dry red wine
2 teaspoons tomato purée
1 teaspoon dried Herbes de Provence
1 bay leaf
450 g (1 lb) frozen leaf spinach
1 teaspoon grated nutmeg
1 × 200 g (7 oz) heart-shaped Neufchâtel cheese
Topping:
15 g (½ oz) butter
1 garlic clove, peeled and crushed
350 g (12 oz) tomatoes, skinned, seeded and chopped
¼ teaspoon finely chopped fresh basil (optional)

Preparation time: 30 minutes
Cooking time: about 25 minutes

If it is difficult to find heart-shaped Neufchâtel cheese, round Camembert can be substituted.

1. Heat the butter and oil in a frying pan. Add the veal escalopes with salt and pepper to taste and brown quickly on both sides. Remove and keep warm.
2. Add the onion to the pan juices and cook until softened. Add the flour and cook for 1 minute.
3. Gradually add the stock and wine, stirring well to make a smooth sauce. Add the tomato purée, herbs, bay leaf and salt and pepper to taste. Add the veal and cook over a gentle heat for about 10 minutes.
4. Meanwhile, cook the spinach according to the packet instructions. Drain and mix with the nutmeg. Place round the edge of a flameproof serving dish and keep warm.
5. For the topping, melt the butter in a pan. Add the garlic and tomatoes and simmer gently for 5 minutes. Add the basil if used.
6. Remove the veal escalopes from the sauce and place inside the spinach. Spread the escalopes with the tomato topping.
7. Cut the cheese into four slices, keeping the shape of the heart. Arrange on top of the veal escalopes. Place under a preheated hot grill and cook until the cheese bubbles.
8. Serve at once with the sauce served separately in a jug, discarding the bay leaf.

SPICY LAMB PAPILLOTES

Serves 6
50 g (2 oz) butter
6 lamb loin chops
2 onions, peeled and sliced
2 garlic cloves, peeled and crushed
1 teaspoon ground ginger
1 teaspoon ground allspice
1 teaspoon dried rosemary
2 tablespoons set honey
salt
freshly ground black pepper
To garnish:
sprigs of fresh rosemary
slices of tomato

Preparation time: 5 minutes
Cooking time: about 1 hour
Oven: 190°C, 375°F, Gas Mark 5

1. Melt the butter in a pan. Add the lamb chops and brown quickly on both sides. Remove from the pan with a slotted spoon and reserve.
2. Add the onion and garlic to the pan juices and cook for 3 minutes.
3. Add the ginger, allspice and rosemary, blending well. Cook for 1 minute.
4. Add the honey and salt and pepper to taste and cook for a further 1 minute.
5. Fold six squares of foil in half diagonally, making sure each is large enough to enfold a chop. Trim each foil triangle to a semi-circle. Place each chop on one side of the opened out foil and top each with an equal quantity of the onion mixture. Loosely fold the foil to enclose the meat and onion mixture and seal the edges by crimping them into small pleats to make foil papillotes or parcels, finishing with a little twist at the end.
6. Put on a baking sheet. Place in a preheated oven and cook for 45-50 minutes or until very tender. Serve garnished with fresh rosemary sprigs and slices of tomato.

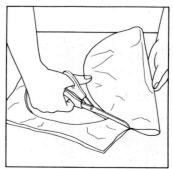

Fold foil in half and cut round in a semi-circle.

Crimp the edges to enclose the mixture, finishing with a twist.

MID-WEEK ROAST CHICKEN

Serves 4-6
25 g (1 oz) rolled oats
50 g (2 oz) fresh brown breadcrumbs
1 small onion, peeled and grated
75 g (3 oz) cooked ham, finely chopped
2 sticks celery, scrubbed and finely chopped
1 tablespoon chopped fresh parsley
½ teaspoon dried thyme
salt
freshly ground black pepper
1 egg, beaten
1.75 kg (4 lb) roasting chicken
25 g (1 oz) butter

Preparation time: 20 minutes
Cooking time: 1½-2 hours
Oven: 190°C, 375°F, Gas Mark 5

1. Mix the oats with the breadcrumbs, onion, ham, celery, parsley, thyme and salt and pepper to taste. Bind together to make a stuffing with the beaten egg.
2. Using your hands, carefully lift the skin from the breast of the chicken from the neck end – taking care not to puncture the skin. Push the stuffing under the breast skin and into the neck cavity. Secure the neck skin underneath the bird with wooden cocktail sticks or string. Truss the chicken to a neat shape. Ⓐ
3. Place the chicken in a roasting tin and dot with the butter. Sprinkle generously with salt and pepper.
4. Place in a preheated oven and cook for 1½-2 hours or until cooked through and golden brown.
5. Serve this delicious roast chicken hot or cold.

Ⓐ The stuffing can be prepared up to 24 hours in advance. Chill until required. Stuff the chicken just before cooking, according to the instructions above.

STEAKS WITH GREEN OR PINK PEPPERCORN SAUCE

salt
freshly ground black pepper
4 rump or fillet steaks, about 150 g (5 oz) each
50 g (2 oz) butter
2 tablespoons brandy
150 ml (¼ pint) double cream
2 tablespoons canned or bottled green or pink peppercorns
To garnish:
sprigs of watercress

Preparation time: 5 minutes
Cooking time: 10-15 minutes

1. Sprinkle salt and pepper to taste on both sides of the steaks.
2. Melt the butter in a large frying pan, add the steaks and fry quickly on both sides until browned, about 3-5 minutes each side, according to taste. Pour over the brandy, ignite and allow the flames to die down. Remove the steaks from the pan with a slotted spoon and place on a warmed serving dish.
3. Add the cream and peppercorns to the pan and cook for a 1 minute or until lightly thickened.
4. Spoon over the steaks and garnish with the watercress sprigs.

Steaks with green or pink peppercorn sauce; Duck with Oriental plum sauce

DUCK WITH ORIENTAL PLUM SAUCE

1 × 570 g (1 lb 4 oz) can plums
2 tablespoons tomato ketchup
2 tablespoons black treacle
1 tablespoon wine vinegar
1 teaspoon made mustard
1½ teaspoons Chinese seasoning
1 garlic clove, peeled and crushed
salt
freshly ground black pepper
4 duck portions or 1 × 2.25 kg (5 lb) oven-ready duck,
    quartered

Preparation time: 15 minutes
Cooking time: 1½ hours
Oven: 190°C, 375°F, Gas Mark 5

1. Drain and stone the plums, reserving the juice. Place the plums in a blender goblet with the ketchup, treacle, vinegar, mustard, Chinese seasoning, garlic and salt and pepper to taste. Purée until smooth. Alternatively, mix the ingredients together, heat gently to soften the treacle, then pass through a fine wire sieve.
2. Mix the purée with enough of the plum juice, about 3 tablespoons, to give a mixture with a basting sauce consistency.
3. Place the duck in a roasting tin and brush liberally with the plum sauce. Place in a preheated oven and cook for about 1½ hours until crisp and golden. Baste frequently with the sauce during the cooking time. Serve hot or cold with a crisp salad.

MUSHROOM FRIES WITH STILTON DRESSING

1 × 398 g (14 oz) packet frozen puff pastry, thawed
1 tablespoon lemon juice
1 tablespoon chopped mixed fresh herbs
18 medium button mushrooms, trimmed
oil for deep frying
Dressing:
100 g (4 oz) Stilton cheese, finely grated
5 tablespoons soured cream
5 tablespoons plain unsweetened yogurt
1 tablespoon snipped fresh chives
salt
freshly ground black pepper

Preparation time: 30 minutes
Cooking time: 15-20 minutes

1. Roll out the pastry into a 30 cm (12 inch) square. Cut into 36 (5 cm/2 inch) squares.
2. Dampen the pastry edges with water. Mix the lemon juice and herbs together. Dip each mushroom into the mixture and place on a square of pastry. Cover with the remaining pastry squares, pinching the edges well to seal.
3. Heat the oil in a pan to 180°-190°C/350°-375°F or until a cube of bread browns in 30 seconds. Add the mushroom fries, in batches, and deep fry for about 4-5 minutes until golden and well puffed. Drain on paper towels and keep warm.
4. Meanwhile, cream the Stilton with the soured cream, yogurt, chives and salt and pepper to taste. Serve with the warm mushroom fries.

HAM AND MUSHROOM GOUGÈRE

Serves 4-6
1 tablespoon oil
1 onion, peeled and chopped
100 g (4 oz) button mushrooms, sliced
225 g (8 oz) cooked smoked ham, chopped
salt
freshly ground black pepper
75 g (3 oz) butter
200 ml (7 fl oz) water
100 g (4 oz) plain flour
3 eggs
2 tablespoons fresh white breadcrumbs
75 g (3 oz) Cheddar cheese, grated
1 tablespoon snipped fresh chives

Preparation time: 25 minutes
Cooking time: 40 minutes
Oven: 220°C, 425°F, Gas Mark 7

SAVOURY CREAM PASTA

225 g (8 oz) pasta shells
salt
1 teaspoon oil
25 g (1 oz) butter
100 g (4 oz) mushrooms, sliced
175 g (6 oz) cooked ham, shredded
150 ml (¼ pint) double cream
175 g (6 oz) Cheddar cheese, grated
freshly ground black pepper
1 tablespoon chopped fresh parsley
To garnish:
a few black olives
2 tablespoons grated Parmesan cheese

Preparation time: 10 minutes
Cooking time: about 17-20 minutes

1. Cook the pasta shells in a large saucepan of lightly salted boiling water with the oil according to the packet instructions for 8-12 minutes, until just tender. Drain thoroughly.
2. Melt the butter in a pan. Add the mushrooms and ham and cook for about 5 minutes until softened. Add the drained pasta and toss over a very gentle heat to warm through.
3. Mix the cream with the cheese and salt and pepper to taste. Stir into the pasta mixture with the parsley and toss quickly over a very gentle heat until well coated and lightly thickened.
4. Transfer to a warmed serving dish. Garnish with a few black olives and sprinkle with the Parmesan cheese. Serve at once.

For 2 people, halve the quantities (using 2 size 4 eggs) and reduce the cooking time to about 25 minutes.

1. Heat the oil in a pan. Add the onion and mushrooms and cook for about 5 minutes until softened. Add the ham, salt and pepper. Set aside.
2. Gently heat the butter and water in a pan to melt. Bring to the boil, add the flour, all at once, and beat to a smooth ball that leaves the sides of the pan clean.
3. Cool slightly then beat in the eggs, one at a time.
4. Spread half of this choux paste over the base of a greased ovenproof dish and spoon the remaining choux paste round the edge of the dish. Spoon the ham and mushroom mixture into the centre.
5. Sprinkle evenly with the breadcrumbs and cheese. Place in a preheated oven and cook for about 30 minutes or until well risen and golden brown.
6. Serve at once, sprinkled with the chives.

Mushroom fries with Stilton dressing; Ham and mushroom gougère

BOBOTIE

25 g (1 oz) butter
1 onion, peeled and finely chopped
1 dessert apple, peeled, cored and finely chopped
1 tablespoon mild curry powder
1 tablespoon apricot jam or mango chutney
1 large slice bread, crusts removed
300 ml (½ pint) milk
750 g (1½ lb) lean minced cooked lamb
25 g (1 oz) seedless raisins
1 tablespoon lemon juice
salt
freshly ground black pepper
2 eggs, beaten
few lemon, lime, orange or bay leaves
25 g (1 oz) flaked almonds

Preparation time: 20 minutes
Cooking time: 55 minutes
Oven: 180°C, 350°F, Gas Mark 4

Bobotie is one of South Africa's typical informal dishes, although Malay in origin, and on par in popularity with our Shepherd's pie. It consists of curried minced lamb with a savoury custard topping. Bobotie is the perfect cook ahead dish since it needs little last minute attention.

1. Melt the butter in a pan. Add the onion and apple and cook for about 5 minutes until softened.
2. Add the curry powder and cook for 2 minutes. Stir in the jam or chutney and cook for a further 1 minute. Remove from the heat.
3. Meanwhile, soak the bread in 2-3 tablespoons of the milk. Squeeze to remove any excess moisture then mix with the lamb, onion mixture, raisins, lemon juice and salt and pepper to taste. Place in a 1.5 litre (2½ pint) shallow ovenproof dish and smooth the surface. Ⓐ Ⓕ
4. Beat the eggs with the remaining milk and salt and pepper to taste. Strain over the top of the meat mixture. Top with the leaves and scatter with the almonds (discarding the leaves when serving).
5. Place in a preheated oven and cook for 45 minutes or until the topping is set and golden. Serve hot with fluffy boiled rice, sliced onion, sliced tomatoes, desiccated coconut, chutney and poppadums.

Ⓐ Bobotie can be chilled up to 24 hours in advance. Prepare the topping as above, allowing an extra 5 minutes cooking time if well chilled.
Ⓕ Freeze for up to 3 months. To serve, thaw overnight in the refrigerator or for 6-8 hours at room temperature then proceed as above.

SAUSAGE MEAT TOAD-IN-THE-HOLE WITH TOMATO SAUCE

450 g (1 lb) herby sausage meat or 450 g (1 lb) pork sausage
    meat mixed with 2 teaspoons mixed dried herbs
2 onions, peeled and finely chopped
salt
freshly ground black pepper
3 tablespoons oil
120 g (4½ oz) plain flour
2 eggs
200 ml (7 fl oz) milk
1 garlic clove, peeled and crushed
1 × 400 g (14 oz) can tomatoes, chopped
1 × 141 g (5 oz) can tomato purée
4 tablespoons red wine, beef stock or tomato juice
1 tablespoon brown sugar
1 teaspoon Worcestershire sauce
½ teaspoon dried oregano
½ teaspoon dried basil

Preparation time: 30 minutes
Cooking time: 1 hour
Oven: 200°C, 400°F, Gas Mark 6

1. Mix the sausage meat with one of the chopped onions and salt and pepper to taste, blending well. Divide the mixture into twelve equal portions and shape into small nuggets. Heat 1 tablespoon of the oil in a frying pan and brown the nuggets on all sides. Remove with a slotted spoon.
2. Meanwhile, sift the flour and a pinch of salt into a bowl. Make a well in the centre and add the eggs. Mix, gradually drawing the flour into the eggs, to make a thick paste. Gradually add the milk, beating well to blend and make a smooth batter.
3. Place the remaining oil in a 30 × 23 cm (12 × 9 inch) roasting tin. Add the nuggets, spacing them evenly. Place in a preheated oven and cook for 10 minutes or until the oil sizzles. Add the batter, return to the oven and cook for a further 40 minutes or until well risen and golden.
4. Meanwhile, add the remaining onion to the frying pan juices and cook for about 5 minutes until softened. Add the garlic, tomatoes, tomato purée, red wine, stock or tomato juice, brown sugar, Worcestershire sauce, oregano, basil and salt and pepper to taste, blending well. Bring to the boil, lower the heat and simmer until the toad-in-the-hole is cooked.
5. Serve with the chunky tomato sauce.

Sausage meat toad-in-the-hole with tomato sauce; Continental soufflé surprises

CONTINENTAL SOUFFLÉ SURPRISES

4 small cob rolls
65 g (2½ oz) butter, at room temperature
100 g (4 oz) Continental ham sausage or meat, sliced
40 g (1½ oz) plain flour
200 ml (7 fl oz) milk
2 small eggs (sizes 5, 6), separated
50 g (2 oz) Gruyère cheese, grated
salt
freshly ground black pepper
2 teaspoons chopped fresh mixed herbs
1 small canned pimiento, finely chopped

Preparation time: 25 minutes
Cooking time: 30-40 minutes
Oven: 190°C, 375°F, Gas Mark 5

1. Cut the top off each of the rolls and scoop out the soft bread from inside (use to make breadcrumbs for another dish).
2. Using 25 g (1 oz) of the butter, coat the outside of each roll liberally. Wrap the outer crusts in foil so that they are protected from too much heat but leave the tops exposed.
3. Line the insides of each bread 'nest' with slices of the Continental ham sausage or meat, allowing the slices to peep above the rim of the bread.
4. Melt the remaining butter in a pan. Add the flour and cook for 1 minute, stirring. Gradually add the milk, blending well. Bring to the boil and cook for 2-3 minutes, stirring. Remove from the heat and allow to cool slightly.
5. Add the egg yolks to the basic sauce mixture with the cheese, salt and pepper to taste, herbs and pimiento, blending well.
6. Whisk the egg whites until they stand in stiff peaks. Fold into the soufflé mixture with a metal spoon.
7. Spoon the soufflé mixture equally into the bread 'nests'. Place in a preheated oven and cook for 25-30 minutes or until well risen and golden brown. Serve at once.

CHIPOLATA AND KIDNEY PIES

25 g (1 oz) butter
1 tablespoon oil
20 button onions, peeled
8 lamb's kidneys, cored and sliced
225 g (8 oz) chipolata sausages, cut into bite-sized pieces
1 tablespoon wholemeal flour
300 ml (½ pint) beef stock
175 ml (6 fl oz) dry red wine
225 g (8 oz) small button mushrooms
1 teaspoon chopped fresh thyme
1 teaspoon creamed horseradish
salt
freshly ground black pepper
1 × 398 g (14 oz) packet frozen puff pastry, thawed
beaten egg to glaze

Preparation time: 30 minutes
Cooking time: about 1 hour
Oven: 200°C, 400°F, Gas Mark 6;
then: 180°C, 350°F, Gas Mark 4

1. Melt the butter and oil in a large pan. Add the onions and cook quickly on all sides to brown. Add the kidneys and sausages and cook for about 10 minutes or until lightly browned. Remove with a slotted spoon and set aside.
2. Add the flour to the pan juices and cook for 1 minute. Gradually add the stock and wine, blending well. Add the kidney, sausage and onion mixture with the mushrooms, thyme, horseradish and salt and pepper to taste. Cover and simmer over a gentle heat for about 15-20 minutes. Spoon into four individual pie dishes and allow to cool slightly.
3. Roll out the pastry on a lightly floured surface and cut into four rounds about 4 cm (1½ inches) larger than the pie dishes. Trim a 2.5 cm (1 inch) strip from each and use to line the dampened rim of each dish. Dampen the pastry rims with water and cover with the pastry lids. Trim, seal and flute the edges. Use any pastry trimmings to decorate the pies.
4. Brush with beaten egg to glaze. Place in a preheated oven and cook for 10 minutes. Reduce the oven temperature and cook for a further 15 minutes or until the pies are well risen, golden brown and cooked through. Serve hot with fresh vegetables in season.

Variation:
Chipolata and kidney pies can be given the luxury treatment for special occasions by adding 100 g (4 oz) walnut halves to the basic meat mixture and by replacing half of the red wine with brandy. Prepare and cook as above.

KIDNEYS JAPANESE STYLE

4 tablespoons soy sauce
3 tablespoons dry sherry
2 tablespoons clear honey
300 ml (½ pint) canned beef consommé
1 garlic clove, peeled and crushed
pinch of five spice powder or Chinese seasoning
12 lamb's kidneys, halved and cored
25 g (1 oz) seasoned flour
40 g (1½ oz) butter
1 tablespoon cornflour
salt
freshly ground black pepper
To garnish:
spring onion curls
carrot scrolls or shapes

Preparation time: 25 minutes, plus marinating
Cooking time: 10-12 minutes

1. Mix the soy sauce, sherry, honey, beef consommé, garlic and five spice powder in a bowl. Add the kidneys, tossing well to coat, cover and leave to marinate for 30 minutes.
2. Remove the kidneys with a spoon and pat dry with paper towels. Toss in the seasoned flour to coat.
3. Melt the butter in a deep frying pan. Add the kidneys and cook over a moderate heat for 5 minutes. Remove with a slotted spoon and reserve.
4. Add the marinade to the pan and bring to the boil, stirring constantly. Blend the cornflour with a little water and stir into the sauce, stirring constantly. Cook until lightly thickened.
5. Add the kidneys to the sauce with salt and pepper to taste. Cook for 1-2 minutes or until the kidneys are heated through and cooked but still tender. Serve at once with boiled rice and garnished with spring onion curls and carrot scrolls or decorative shapes.

Kidneys Japanese style look all the more authentic if they are presented with traditional vegetable garnishes. To make *spring onion curls*: trim most of the green tops off the spring onions, thinly slice any remaining green lengthways to the bulb. Chill in iced water to curl. To make *carrot and other vegetable shapes*: slice a peeled carrot, swede or turnip crossways and cut out shapes with a canapé cutter or sharp knife. Traditional shapes include hearts, fish, moons and flowers.

CALF'S LIVER WITH SAGE

50 g (2 oz) butter
1 tablespoon grated onion
4 large thin slices calf's liver, about 90 g (3½ oz) each
3 tablespoons chopped fresh sage
salt
freshly ground black pepper
4 tablespoons oil
750 g (1½ lb) potatoes, peeled and diced
sea salt, to sprinkle
2 tablespoons dry sherry or light meat stock
1 tablespoon chopped fresh parsley (optional)

Preparation time: 15 minutes
Cooking time: about 15 minutes

1. Melt the butter in a frying pan. Add the onion and cook gently for about 5 minutes. Add the liver and cook gently for about 3 minutes until golden on the underside. Turn over, sprinkle generously with sage and salt and pepper, and cook for about 2 minutes until the remaining side is also golden.
2. Meanwhile, heat the oil in a deep frying pan. Add the potatoes and cook for about 10-12 minutes over a moderate heat until golden, crisp and tender. Drain on paper towels. Sprinkle with a little sea salt.
3. Remove the calf's liver from the pan with a slotted spoon and arrange on a warmed serving plate with the pan-fried potatoes.
4. Stir the sherry or stock into the liver pan juices. Cook for 1 minute to reduce slightly then pour over the cooked liver. Sprinkle with chopped parsley if used and serve at once with vegetables in season.

Calf's liver with sage; Kidneys Japanese style

OCEAN PIE

450 g (1 lb) mixed white fish (eg. cod, coley, haddock, hake, sole or whiting), skinned and boned
300 ml (½ pint) milk
salt
freshly ground white pepper
100 g (4 oz) peeled prawns
75 g (3 oz) butter
25 g (1 oz) plain flour
1 tablespoon chopped fresh parsley
2 teaspoons grated lemon rind
750 g (1½ lb) potatoes, peeled
100 g (4 oz) Cheddar cheese, grated
To garnish:
lemon butterflies
sprigs of parsley

Preparation time: 20 minutes
Cooking time: about 45 minutes
Oven: 190°C, 375°F, Gas Mark 5

1. Place the fish, milk and salt and pepper to taste in a pan. Bring to the boil, lower the heat and poach the fish for about 5 minutes until tender. Drain the fish, reserving the milk, and flake into bite-sized pieces.
2. Mix the flaked fish with the prawns and place in a 900 ml (1½ pint) shallow ovenproof dish.
3. Melt 25 g (1 oz) of the butter in a pan. Add the flour and cook for 1 minute, stirring. Gradually add the reserved milk to make a smooth sauce. Bring to the boil and cook for 2 minutes, stirring. Stir in the parsley and lemon and pour over the fish. Keep warm.
4. Meanwhile, cook the potatoes in a pan of lightly salted boiling water for about 20 minutes, until tender. Drain and mash to a purée with the remaining butter. Stir in half of the cheese, blending well. Pipe or spoon attractively on top of the fish mixture and sprinkle with the remaining cheese. Ⓐ Ⓕ
5. Place in a preheated oven and cook for 20-25 minutes or until golden brown and crisp. Serve garnished with lemon butterflies and parsley sprigs.

Ⓐ Make up to 24 hours ahead and chill. Cook for an additional 10 minutes in a preheated oven.
Ⓕ Freeze for up to 3 months. Reheat from frozen, uncovered, in a preheated oven for about 1½ hours. Alternatively, thaw overnight in the refrigerator or for 6-8 hours at room temperature, then cook in a preheated oven for 30-35 minutes.

HONEY AND VEGETABLE JULIENNE MACKEREL

Serves 2
2 mackerel, about 450 g (1 lb) each, cleaned and heads removed
2 tablespoons clear honey
1 carrot, peeled and cut into thin julienne strips
1 stick celery, scrubbed and cut into thin julienne strips
1 × 5 cm (2 inch) slice fresh ginger root, peeled and cut into thin julienne strips
salt
freshly ground black pepper
1 tablespoon wine vinegar
1 tablespoon soy sauce

Preparation time: 15 minutes
Cooking time: 30 minutes
Oven: 190°C, 375°F, Gas Mark 5

1. Place the mackerel on a large piece of greased foil. Brush with the honey and sprinkle with the carrot, celery and ginger root. Sprinkle with salt and pepper to taste, the wine vinegar and soy sauce.
2. Fold over the foil to enclose the fish completely and put on a baking sheet. Place in a preheated oven and cook for 30 minutes or until tender.
3. Remove from the foil to serve.

TROUT AND TARRAGON

4 trout, cleaned
100 ml (3½ fl oz) dry white wine
2 tablespoons water
1 tablespoon finely chopped onion
1 lemon, very thinly sliced
2 tablespoons chopped fresh parsley
2 tablespoons chopped fresh tarragon
150 ml (¼ pint) double cream
salt
freshly ground black pepper

Preparation time: 10 minutes
Cooking time: 12-15 minutes

1. Place the trout in a frying pan with a lid and add the wine, water, onion, lemon slices and half of the herbs. Bring to a simmer, cover and poach for 10 minutes or until the trout is tender.
2. Remove the trout and lemon slices and arrange decoratively on a warmed serving dish.
3. Add the cream to the pan, increase the heat and cook until thickened. Add salt and pepper to taste and spoon over the trout.
4. Sprinkle with the remaining parsley and tarragon, and serve at once.

Honey and vegetable julienne mackerel; Ocean pie

MALMSEY MUSHROOMS WITH HAM

100 g (4 oz) butter
225 g (8 oz) very small button mushrooms
225 g (8 oz) cooked ham, finely chopped
4 tablespoons Malmsey Madeira
4 tablespoons double cream
100 g (4 oz) mature Cheddar cheese, grated
1 tablespoon chopped mixed fresh herbs
4 slices white bread
a little paprika pepper
To garnish:
sprigs of parsley or coriander

Preparation time: 15 minutes
Cooking time: about 15 minutes

This dish is a speciality of an award-winning restaurant near Amersham in Buckinghamshire. The secret of its success lies in choosing baby button mushrooms that are meltingly tender and rich Malmsey Madeira.

1. Melt 50 g (2 oz) of the butter in a pan. Add the mushrooms and cook for about 4 minutes until just tender. Add the ham and cook for a further 2 minutes.
2. Add the Madeira and bring to the boil. Cook for 1 minute to reduce the juices slightly. Add the cream, blending well, and cook gently for about 2 minutes.
3. Spoon into a large shallow flameproof dish or four small individual flameproof dishes and sprinkle with the cheese.
4. Meanwhile, blend the remaining butter with the herbs and use to spread on both sides of the bread.
5. Place the mushroom dish under a preheated hot grill and cook until bubbly. Remove from the heat, sprinkle with paprika and garnish with sprigs of parsley or coriander. Keep warm.
6. Toast the bread on both sides until golden. Cut into thick fingers and serve with the mushrooms.

Malmsey mushrooms with ham served with fingers of toast; Crinkly bacon stuffed potatoes

CRINKLY BACON STUFFED POTATOES

4 large potatoes, scrubbed
225 g (8 oz) streaky bacon, rinded and chopped
100 g (4 oz) button mushrooms, sliced
8 tablespoons soured cream
salt
freshly ground black pepper
2 tablespoons snipped fresh chives
To garnish:
4 rashers streaky bacon, rinded

Preparation time: 15 minutes
Cooking time: about 1 hour 20 minutes
Oven: 190°C, 375°F, Gas Mark 5

1. Prick the potatoes. Place in a preheated oven and cook for about 1 hour until crisp, golden and tender.
2. Meanwhile, fry the bacon in its own fat until crisp and golden. Add the mushrooms and cook for a further 5 minutes.

3. Slice off the tops of the potatoes and scoop out the soft potato into a bowl.
4. Mix the potato flesh with the mushroom and bacon mixture, 4 tablespoons of the soured cream and salt and pepper to taste. Fold in 1 tablespoon of the snipped chives. Pile back high into the potato skins. Ⓐ
5. Return to the oven and bake for a further 5-10 minutes.
6. Meanwhile, pleat the bacon rashers on to a skewer. Place under a preheated hot grill and cook until golden.
7. Remove the potatoes from the oven. Spoon over the remaining soured cream, top with the pleated bacon rashers and sprinkle with the remaining chives.
8. Serve at once with a mixed side salad.

Ⓐ The potatoes can be prepared up to 24 hours in advance. Chill until required. Reheat in a preheated oven for 20-25 minutes then proceed as above to garnish.

ONE-POT DISHES

FRENCH ONION SOUP WITH CHEESE BÂTONS

50 g (2 oz) butter
1 tablespoon oil
450 g (1 lb) onions, peeled and thinly sliced
½ teaspoon sugar
2 tablespoons plain flour
1 litre (1¾ pints) rich beef stock
salt
freshly ground black pepper
4 thick slices bread
1 garlic clove, peeled and halved
100 g (4 oz) Gruyère cheese, grated
2 tablespoons brandy (optional)

Preparation time: 10 minutes
Cooking time: 45 minutes

1. Heat the butter and oil in a large heavy-based saucepan. Add the onions, cover and cook over a moderate heat for 20 minutes.
2. Increase the heat, stir in the sugar and cook, uncovered, until the onions caramelize and turn a rich golden colour, stirring frequently.
3. Add the flour and cook until golden. Gradually add the stock, blending well. Add salt and pepper to taste, bring to the boil, lower the heat, cover and simmer for 20 minutes.
4. Meanwhile, rub the bread slices with the cut side of the garlic clove. Place under a preheated hot grill and toast on one side. Turn over and sprinkle with the cheese. Grill until golden and bubbly. Cut the bread slices into thick strips or bâtons.
5. Add the brandy to the soup, if used, and ladle into warmed soup bowls. Add the cheese bâtons and serve at once.

NASI GORENG

Serves 4-6
50 g (2 oz) butter
450 g (1 lb) boned shoulder of pork, cut into bite-sized strips
2 onions, peeled and sliced
225 g (8 oz) long-grain rice
1 red pepper, cored, seeded and chopped
50 g (2 oz) shelled peas
50 g (2 oz) cucumber, chopped
50 g (2 oz) carrot, grated
4 tablespoons soy sauce
1 teaspoon curry powder
pinch of five spice powder
salt
freshly ground black pepper
Omelette:
1 egg
1 teaspoon cold water
salt
freshly ground black pepper
15 g (½ oz) butter
To garnish:
2 tomatoes, cut into wedges
spring onion curls (page 58)

Preparation time: 15 minutes
Cooking time: about 30 minutes

Nasi Goreng is an Indonesian dish which can be kept warm and covered, for up to 30 minutes after cooking.

1. Melt the butter in a pan. Add the pork and fry for about 5-8 minutes until golden. Add the onions and cook for a further 10 minutes.
2. Meanwhile, cook the rice in a pan of boiling salted water according to the packet instructions for about 15 minutes. Drain thoroughly.
3. Add the pepper, peas, cucumber and carrot to the pork mixture and cook for a further 5 minutes. Stir in the soy sauce, curry powder, five spice powder and salt and pepper to taste, blending well. Add the rice, tossing well to mix and reheat gently. Ⓕ
4. For the omelette, beat the egg with the water and salt and pepper to taste. Melt the butter in a small omelette pan and add the egg. Cook gently until the underside is golden. Turn and brown the second side. Slide on to a plate and cut into wide strips.
5. Put the rice mixture on a warmed serving dish and top with a lattice of omelette strips. Garnish with tomato wedges and spring onion curls.

Ⓕ Freeze for up to 3 months. Thaw overnight in the refrigerator or for 4-6 hours at room temperature. Reheat gently in a non-stick pan for 10-15 minutes. Prepare the omelette and garnish as above.

French onion soup with cheese bâtons; Nasi goreng

CHUNKY GAZPACHO

2 small slices brown bread, crusts removed
600 ml (1 pint) tomato juice
2 garlic cloves, peeled
½ cucumber, peeled and finely chopped
1 green pepper, cored, seeded and chopped
1 red pepper, cored, seeded and chopped
1 large onion, peeled and finely chopped
750 g (1½ lb) tomatoes, skinned, seeded and chopped
4 tablespoons olive oil
2 tablespoons red wine vinegar
salt
freshly ground black pepper
¼ teaspoon dried marjoram
¼ teaspoon dried basil
1 tablespoon chopped fresh parsley
To garnish:
croûtons
sliced stuffed green olives
chopped cucumber
chopped green and red peppers
onion rings or chopped spring onions

Preparation time: 25 minutes, plus chilling

A classic Spanish main course soup, Gazpacho makes a refreshing light supper or lunch dish. Guests sprinkle their bowls of soup with a little of each garnish before eating.
1. Chop the bread coarsely and place in a blender goblet with the tomato juice and garlic. Allow to stand for 5 minutes then purée until smooth. Alternatively, leave the mixture to stand then mash thoroughly.
2. Add the cucumber, peppers, onion, tomatoes, olive oil, vinegar, salt and pepper to taste, marjoram and basil, blending well. Transfer to a chilled soup tureen or serving dish.
3. Chill thoroughly for about 1 hour. Sprinkle with parsley and serve with small bowls of croûtons, olives, cucumber, peppers and onion. Accompany with crusty French bread.

Chunky gazpacho is all the more flavoursome if served with a selection of unusual croûtons.

Deep fry cubes or shapes of bread in hot oil for 1 minute until crisp and golden. Drain them on paper towels then toss in coarse sea salt, freshly grated lemon rind, finely chopped fresh herbs, garlic granules. finely grated Parmesan cheese, onion salt or steak pepper for delicious results.

MAIN COURSE MINESTRONE

350 g (12 oz) streaky bacon, rinded and diced
2 garlic cloves, peeled and crushed
4 celery sticks, trimmed and chopped
4 carrots, peeled and sliced
2 onions, peeled and chopped
2 potatoes, peeled and diced
1 × 400 g (14 oz) can tomatoes
300 ml (½ pint) chicken stock
1 bouquet garni
1 teaspoon chopped fresh basil
salt
freshly ground black pepper
1 × 411 g (14½ oz) can haricot beans, drained
50 g (2 oz) spaghetti
225 g (8 oz) Italian ham sausage, sliced
225 g (8 oz) cabbage, shredded
2 courgettes, sliced
100 g (4 oz) mangetout or French beans, trimmed
4-6 tablespoons grated Parmesan cheese
To garnish:
sprigs of fresh basil (optional)

Preparation time: 25 minutes
Cooking time: 40 minutes

1. Place the bacon in a large flameproof casserole and cook until the fat runs and the bacon is crisp. Add the garlic, celery, carrots, onions and potatoes and cook for 5 minutes, stirring frequently.
2. Add the tomatoes, stock, bouquet garni, basil and salt and pepper to taste. Cover and simmer for 20 minutes.
3. Add the haricot beans, spaghetti, broken into small pieces, ham sausage, cabbage, courgettes and mangetout or French beans. Cover and cook for a further 10 minutes.
4. Remove and discard the bouquet garni. Ladle the soup into a warmed soup tureen or soup bowls. Ⓐ
5. Sprinkle thickly with Parmesan cheese and garnish with a few sprigs of fresh basil, if used.

Ⓐ Store in the refrigerator for up to 48 hours. Reheat gently for 10-15 minutes in a saucepan.

FROM THE LEFT: Chunky gazpacho with garnishes served separately; Main course minestrone; Fish chowder Provence style

FISH CHOWDER PROVENCE STYLE

Serves 4-6

3 tablespoons oil
450 g (1 lb) onions, peeled and grated
1 garlic clove, peeled and crushed
1 × 850 g (28 oz) can tomatoes
1 bouquet garni
4 medium floury potatoes, peeled and cut into bite-sized cubes
about 20 small black olives, stoned
2 tablespoons capers
300 ml (½ pint) tomato juice
600 ml (1 pint) light chicken, vegetable or fish stock
salt
freshly ground black pepper
750 g (1½ lb) white fish (eg. coley, cod, haddock, sole or whiting), skinned, boned and cut into bite-sized cubes
3 tablespoons finely chopped fresh parsley

Preparation time: 20 minutes
Cooking time: 30-35 minutes

1. Heat the oil in a large pan. Add the onions and garlic and fry gently for about 5 minutes or until lightly browned.
2. Add the tomatoes with their juice and the bouquet garni. Bring to the boil, lower the heat and simmer for 5 minutes, stirring frequently to break up the tomatoes.
3. Add the potatoes, olives, capers, tomato juice, stock and salt and pepper to taste. Cook, uncovered, for 10-15 minutes or until the potatoes are almost cooked. Ⓐ
4. Add the fish and simmer gently, uncovered, for about 5 minutes, until the fish is tender.
5. Remove and discard the bouquet garni. Add the parsley and adjust the seasoning, if necessary. Transfer to a warmed serving dish or tureen. Serve at once with thick wedges of crusty bread.

Ⓐ The fish chowder can be prepared up to a day in advance to stage 3. Chill until required. Reheat gently until hot, add the fish and parsley and complete the cooking as above.

LATTICE-TOPPED COTTAGE PIE

Savoury mince:
2 tablespoons oil
1 rasher bacon, rinded and diced
1 onion, peeled and chopped
1 garlic clove, peeled and chopped (optional)
1 celery stick, chopped
1 large carrot, peeled and chopped
450 g (1 lb) lean minced beef
1 × 225 g (8 oz) can tomatoes, chopped
4 tablespoons dry red wine or rich beef stock
salt
freshly ground black pepper
pinch of grated nutmeg
Lattice topping:
350 g (12 oz) potatoes, peeled
225 g (8 oz) swede or parsnips, peeled
40 g (1½ oz) butter
4 tablespoons single cream
3 tablespoons grated Cheshire cheese
To garnish:
slices of tomato
sprigs of parsley

Preparation time: 25 minutes
Cooking time: 50 minutes
Oven: 220°C, 425°F, Gas Mark 7

The basis for this pie is a good savoury mince — endlessly versatile for a bolognese sauce or a lasagne filling too. The secret in making a good savoury mince is in the quality of the beef you buy. Always choose the very best quality or buy a piece of chuck steak and mince it at home, or ask the butcher to do it for you.

1. For the topping, cook the potatoes and swede or parsnip in boiling salted water until tender.
2. Meanwhile, heat the oil in a large pan. Add the bacon, onion, garlic, celery and carrot and fry over a moderate heat for 5 minutes.
3. Add the beef and cook for about 10 minutes until lightly browned.
4. Add the tomatoes, wine or stock and salt, pepper and nutmeg to taste. Simmer over a gentle heat for about 15 minutes or until thick and bubbly. Spoon into an ovenproof dish. Ⓐ Ⓕ
5. Drain and mash the potatoes and swede or parsnip with the butter, cream, cheese and salt and pepper to taste until smooth. Spoon into a piping bag fitted with a large star-shaped nozzle and pipe a lattice over the top of the meat. Ⓕ
6. Place in a preheated oven and cook for 20 minutes or until golden and crisp. Serve garnished with tomato slices and parsley sprigs.

Ⓐ The savoury mince can be prepared up to 48 hours ahead if stored in the refrigerator. Reheat gently to use, or cook with the topping for an additional 10 minutes.
Ⓕ The savoury mince can be frozen for up to 3 months. Thaw overnight in the refrigerator or for 4-6 hours at room temperature.
   Alternatively, freeze the pie complete. Reheat from frozen, uncovered, in a preheated moderately hot oven (200°C, 400°F, Gas Mark 6) for about 1½ hours.

HAM AND POTATO GRATIN

Serves 4-6
750 g (1½ lb) potatoes, peeled and very thinly sliced
225 g (8 oz) ham sausage, sliced
2 onions, peeled and sliced
175 g (6 oz) Cheddar cheese, grated
salt
freshly ground black pepper
1 teaspoon grated nutmeg
2 eggs
300 ml (½ pint) milk
3 tablespoons double cream
25 g (1 oz) butter
To garnish:
sprigs of parsley or celery leaves

Preparation time: 15 minutes
Cooking time: 1½ hours
Oven: 160°C, 325°F, Gas Mark 3

FROM THE TOP: Lattice-topped cottage pie; Ham and potato gratin

1. Fill a medium ovenproof dish with alternate layers of potato, ham sausage, onion and cheese, adding salt, pepper and nutmeg between each layer.
2. Beat the eggs with the milk and cream and pour over the dish. Dot with the butter. Place in a preheated oven and cook for 1½ hours or until cooked and golden brown.
3. Serve at once straight from the dish, garnished with parsley sprigs or celery leaves. Accompany the dish with a mixed side salad.

Variations:
Tongue and potato gratin: use 225 g (8 oz) sliced cooked tongue instead of the ham sausage.
Garlic sausage and potato gratin: use 225 g (8 oz) sliced garlic sausage instead of the ham sausage.
Bacon and potato gratin: use 225 g (8 oz) crispy-fried chopped bacon instead of the ham sausage.

CHICKEN WITH BACON DUMPLINGS

2 tablespoons oil
1.5 kg (3¼ lb) fresh chicken, jointed into 8 pieces
350 g (12 oz) button onions, peeled
1 garlic clove, peeled and crushed (optional)
25 g (1 oz) plain flour
600 ml (1 pint) chicken stock
1 bay leaf
2 teaspoons dried mixed herbs
salt
freshly ground black pepper
175 g (6 oz) button mushrooms
Bacon dumplings:
100 g (4 oz) self-raising flour
15 g (½ oz) butter
50 g (2 oz) shredded suet
50 g (2 oz) streaky bacon, rinded and finely chopped
½ small onion, peeled and finely chopped
pinch of dried mixed herbs
1 small egg (sizes 5, 6), beaten
milk to mix

Preparation time: 25 minutes
Cooking time: about 1 hour

1. Heat the oil in a large flameproof casserole. Add the chicken and fry for about 10 minutes until golden. Remove with a slotted spoon and reserve.
2. Add the onions and garlic, if used, to the pan juices and cook for 5 minutes or until golden. Remove with a slotted spoon and reserve.
3. Add the flour to the pan juices and cook for 1 minute, stirring constantly. Gradually add the stock, blending well. Return the chicken and onion mixture to the pan with the bay leaf, herbs, salt and pepper. Cover and cook over a gentle heat for 30 minutes. Ⓕ
4. Meanwhile for the dumplings, sift the flour and a pinch of salt into a mixing bowl. Rub in the butter. Mix in the suet, bacon, onion and dried herbs, blending well. Bind together with the beaten egg and milk to a soft dough. Roll into 8 small balls.
5. Remove and discard the bay leaf from the chicken casserole. Add the button mushrooms, mixing well. Top with the prepared dumplings, cover and cook over a gentle heat for 20 minutes.

Ⓕ Freeze for up to 3 months. Thaw overnight in the refrigerator or for 6-8 hours at room temperature. Reheat gently for 10 minutes, add the freshly-prepared dumplings and mushrooms and cook for a further 20 minutes.

Variation:
Parsley and lemon dumplings: add 1½ tablespoons chopped fresh parsley and the grated rind and juice of 1 lemon to the mixture instead of bacon and herbs.

BUBBLING MOROCCAN CHICKEN

4 tablespoons set honey
1 teaspoon curry powder
½ teaspoon freshly ground black pepper
1 teaspoon salt
pinch of ground allspice
1.5 kg (3¼ lb) fresh chicken, jointed into 8 pieces
1 lemon, thinly sliced
300 ml (½ pint) water
50 g (2 oz) butter
300 ml (½ pint) chicken stock
50 g (2 oz) raisins
chopped fresh parsley
To serve:
pitta bread

Preparation time: 15 minutes, plus marinating
Cooking time: 40-50 minutes

1. Blend 2 tablespoons of the honey with the curry powder, pepper, salt and allspice. Spread over the jointed chicken in a bowl, cover and leave to marinate overnight. Ⓐ
2. Drain the marinade from the chicken into a saucepan. Add the lemon slices and water and cook for 10 minutes over a gentle heat.
3. Meanwhile, melt the butter and remaining honey in a flameproof casserole. Add the chicken pieces and cook for about 15-20 minutes to a deep golden brown on all sides.
4. Add the lemon marinade, stock and raisins, blending well. Bring to the boil, lower the heat, cover and simmer for 15-20 minutes. Ⓕ
5. Taste and adjust the seasoning, if necessary. Sprinkle with chopped parsley and serve hot with warm pitta bread.

Ⓐ The marinated chicken can be prepared in the morning or a day in advance. Cover and keep chilled.
Ⓕ Freeze for up to 3 months. Thaw overnight in the refrigerator or for 6-8 hours at room temperature. Reheat gently for about 20 minutes.

Chicken with bacon dumplings; Chicken Catalan

CHICKEN CATALAN

Serves 6

6 tablespoons olive oil
6 small chicken breasts, skinned and boned
3 onions, peeled and sliced
2 garlic cloves, peeled and crushed
450 g (1 lb) long-grain rice
1-2 tablespoons tomato purée
½-1 teaspoon ground turmeric
1.2 litres (2 pints) hot chicken stock
1 teaspoon paprika pepper
salt
freshly ground black pepper
100 g (4 oz) garlic sausage, skinned and cut into bite-sized
    pieces
1 green pepper, cored, seeded and sliced
1 red pepper, cored, seeded and sliced
100 g (4 oz) stuffed green olives
1 tablespoon chopped fresh parsley

Preparation time: 30 minutes
Cooking time: about 1 hour

1. Heat 3 tablespoons of the oil in a large flameproof casserole. Add the chicken breasts and cook for about 15 minutes until lightly browned on both sides. Remove with a slotted spoon and keep warm.
2. Add the onions and garlic to the pan juices and cook for 2-3 minutes or until softened.
3. Add the remaining oil and the rice to the casserole and cook until the rice turns a light golden colour.
4. Add the tomato purée, turmeric, stock, paprika and salt and pepper to taste, blending well. Bring to the boil then add the chicken, garlic sausage and peppers, pressing them well down into the rice mixture. Lower the heat and simmer for about 30 minutes or until the rice is just tender, stirring occasionally.
5. Add the olives and cook for a further 2-3 minutes to warm through. Sprinkle with the parsley and serve straight from the dish.

RABBIT AND SAUSAGE PIES

25 g (1 oz) lard
450 g (1 lb) boneless rabbit meat, cubed
2 tablespoons plain flour
225 g (8 oz) button mushrooms
225 g (8 oz) button onions, peeled
1 garlic clove, peeled and crushed
100 ml (3½ fl oz) port
300 ml (½ pint) light meat stock
12 juniper berries, crushed
350 g (12 oz) sausage meat
2 tablespoons chopped fresh sage
2 tablespoons made mild mustard
salt
freshly ground black pepper
Cobbler topping:
225 g (8 oz) self-raising flour
50 g (2 oz) butter or margarine
1 teaspoon chopped fresh or ½ teaspoon dried sage
about 6 tablespoons milk
milk or beaten egg to glaze

Preparation time: 30 minutes
Cooking time: 50-55 minutes
Oven: 230°C, 450°F, Gas Mark 8

1. Melt the lard in a pan. Toss the rabbit in the flour to coat. Add to the pan and brown on all sides for about 5 minutes. Remove with a slotted spoon and reserve.

2. Add the mushrooms, onions and garlic to the pan juices. Fry until lightly browned.
3. Stir in the port, stock, juniper berries and rabbit, blending well. Cover and cook over a gentle heat for 10 minutes.
4. Mix the sausage meat with the sage, mustard and salt and pepper to taste. Shape into 8 balls and add to the rabbit mixture. Cook over a gentle heat for a further 5 minutes. Taste and adjust the seasoning if necessary.
5. For the cobbler topping, sift the flour and a pinch of salt into a bowl. Rub in the butter or margarine until the mixture resembles fine breadcrumbs. Stir in the sage and mix to a soft but manageable dough with the milk. Roll out the dough on a lightly floured surface to about 2 cm (¾ inch) thick and cut into rounds, using a 5 cm (2 inch) plain or fluted scone cutter.
6. Spoon the rabbit mixture evenly into four individual pie dishes. Arrange the cobbler rounds on top, overlapping slightly. Brush with milk or beaten egg to glaze. Place in a preheated oven and cook for 25-30 minutes.

Variations:
Onion cobbler topping: prepare the cobbler topping and lay an onion slice on the top of each, pressing down firmly to secure. Glaze and bake as above.
Sesame cobbler topping: prepare the cobbler topping as above. Glaze and sprinkle with sesame seeds. Bake as above.

LIVER AND BACON WITH LEMON AND WINE SAUCE

40 g (1½ oz) butter
6 rashers back bacon, rinded and halved
450 g (1 lb) lamb's liver, thinly sliced
seasoned flour to coat
4 tablespoons dry red wine
150 ml (¼ pint) meat stock
4 tablespoons lemon juice
salt
freshly ground black pepper
2 teaspoons cornflour (optional)
To garnish:
chopped fresh parsley
twists of lemon

Preparation time: 10 minutes
Cooking time: 25 minutes

1. Melt the butter in a deep, heavy-based frying pan. Add the bacon and fry until golden and crisp. Remove with a slotted spoon and reserve.
2. Meanwhile, coat the liver in seasoned flour. Add to the pan juices and quickly brown on both sides for about 5 minutes altogether. Add the wine, stock, lemon juice and bacon. Cover and cook over a gentle heat for about 10-15 minutes or until tender.
3. Add salt and pepper to taste, blending well. Thicken the sauce with the cornflour dissolved in a little cold water, if wished.
4. Serve at once, garnished with chopped fresh parsley and twists of lemon. Serve with a green vegetable and boiled rice.

Rabbit and sausage pies; Liver and bacon with lemon and wine sauce

PORK AND MANGO CURRY

Serves 4-6

750 g (1½ lb) pork fillet, cut into 2.5 cm (1 inch) cubes
25 g (1 oz) plain flour
2 tablespoons oil
1 Spanish onion, peeled and thickly sliced
2 small green or red peppers, cored, seeded and sliced
1 teaspoon turmeric
2 teaspoons salt
1 tablespoon garam masala or curry powder
1 teaspoon ground cumin
1 teaspoon ground ginger
½ teaspoon chilli seasoning
5 medium tomatoes, peeled, seeded and chopped
2 teaspoons tomato purée
450 ml (¾ pint) light meat stock
750 g (1½ lb) small new potatoes, scrubbed or peeled
1 × 425 g (15 oz) can mango slices, drained,
    or 2 large mangoes, peeled, stoned and sliced

Preparation time: 20 minutes
Cooking time: 30 minutes

1. Toss the pork in the flour to coat. Heat the oil in a flameproof casserole. Add the pork and fry for about 5 minutes until golden. Add the onion and peppers and cook for a further 3 minutes.
2. Add the turmeric, salt, garam masala or curry powder, cumin, ginger and chilli seasoning. Cook for 1 minute, stirring constantly.
3. Add the tomatoes, tomato purée and stock, blending well. Add the potatoes, cover and cook for 15 minutes over a gentle heat, stirring occasionally. Add the mango slices and cook for a further 5 minutes until the potatoes are tender. 𝔽
4. Serve the pork and mango curry alone or with a selection of accompaniments such as boiled rice, sliced bananas dipped in lemon juice, desiccated coconut, mango chutney, poppadums, chopped cucumber in plain unsweetened yogurt or a crisp green salad.

𝔽 Freeze for up to 3 months. Thaw overnight in the refrigerator or for 6-8 hours at room temperature. Reheat gently for about 10-15 minutes.

STIR-FRY BEEF AND VEGETABLES

350 g (12 oz) flash fry or quick fry steak
4 tablespoons oil
225 g (8 oz) carrots, peeled and cut into thin julienne strips
1 red or yellow pepper, cored, seeded and sliced
1 bunch spring onions, trimmed and sliced into 2.5 cm
    (1 inch) lengths
1 × 293 g (10 oz) can miniature corn on the cob, drained
1 garlic clove, peeled and crushed
1 teaspoon cornflour
6 tablespoons red wine or dry cider
2 tablespoons soy sauce
150 ml (¼ pint) beef stock
salt
freshly ground black pepper
100 g (4 oz) frozen peas, thawed
175 g (6 oz) bean-sprouts
To garnish:
julienne strips of spring onion

Preparation time: 15 minutes
Cooking time: 12-14 minutes

1. Slice the beef into thin strips across the grain. Heat 2 tablespoons of the oil in a large frying pan or wok, add the beef and stir-fry over a high heat for 2-3 minutes. Remove from the pan with a slotted spoon and keep warm.
2. Add the remaining oil to the pan and heat until hot. Add the carrots, pepper, onions, corn on the cob and garlic. Stir-fry over a high heat for 3-4 minutes.
3. Dissolve the cornflour with the wine or cider and stir in with the soy sauce and stock, blending well. Bring to the boil, stirring constantly. Add salt and pepper to taste.
4. Add the peas, beef and bean-sprouts and stir-fry for 2 minutes to heat through.
5. Serve at once with green noodles, boiled rice or fluffy cooked dumplings (page 70). Cook the dumplings for 12-15 minutes in about 300 ml (½ pint) boiling chicken or beef stock. Garnish with spring onion.

Most aubergines contain the substance solanin, which gives the flesh a slightly bitter taste when it is not fully ripe.

To remove this, it is advisable to sprinkle the sliced flesh with a little salt and lemon juice before cooking. Leave to stand for 30 minutes, during which time the bitter juices will be drawn from the flesh. Rinse and dry before use.

CLOCKWISE FROM THE TOP: Ratatouille and aubergine moussaka; Stir-fry beef and vegetables; Pork and mango curry with accompaniments

RATATOUILLE AND AUBERGINE MOUSSAKA

6 tablespoons oil
1 onion, peeled and chopped
350 g (12 oz) lean minced beef
2 teaspoons tomato purée
1 × 396 g (14 oz) can ratatouille
salt
freshly ground black pepper
2 medium aubergines, thinly sliced
300 ml (½ pint) plain unsweetened yogurt
2 eggs, beaten
2-3 tablespoons grated Parmesan cheese

Preparation time: 20 minutes
Cooking time: about 45 minutes
Oven: 190°C, 375°F, Gas Mark 5

1. Heat 2 tablespoons of the oil in a pan. Add the onion and fry for about 5 minutes or until golden.
2. Add the beef and cook for about 5 minutes until lightly browned. Stir in the tomato purée and rata-taouille, blending well. Add salt and pepper to taste and simmer over a gentle heat for 5 minutes.
3. Meanwhile, heat the remaining oil in a pan and fry the aubergine slices until lightly browned. Drain on paper towels.
4. Layer the beef mixture and aubergine slices in an ovenproof dish. Ⓐ
5. Beat the yogurt with the eggs and salt and pepper to taste. Spoon over the moussaka and sprinkle with the Parmesan cheese.
6. Place in a preheated oven and cook for about 25-30 minutes until golden and bubbly. Serve hot.

Ⓐ Can be prepared a day in advance up to stage 5. Chill until required. Cover with the egg and yogurt topping and Parmesan cheese. Bake in a preheated oven for about 30-35 minutes until golden.

SUMMER TIME PORK POT

2 tablespoons oil
1 onion, peeled and sliced
450 g (1 lb) pork fillet or tenderloin, cubed
1 × 400 g (14 oz) can tomatoes
4 small leeks, cleaned and sliced
4 small courgettes, sliced
1 teaspoon finely chopped fresh basil
salt
freshly ground black pepper
450 g (1 lb) potatoes, peeled and sliced
100 g (4 oz) Cheddar cheese, grated
To garnish:
sprigs of parsley

Preparation time: 20 minutes
Cooking time: 1 hour
Oven: 180°C, 350°F, Gas Mark 4

1. Heat the oil in a flameproof casserole. Add the onion and pork and brown on all sides for about 10 minutes.
2. Add the tomatoes, leeks, courgettes, basil and salt and pepper to taste, blending well. Remove from the heat and layer the potatoes on top of the meat and vegetable mixture.
3. Place, covered, in a preheated oven and cook for 30 minutes.
4. Sprinkle with the cheese and bake, uncovered, for a further 20 minutes. Serve garnished with parsley sprigs.

SWEET AND SOUR PORK BALLS

500 g (1¼ lb) lean minced pork
50 g (2 oz) fresh wholemeal breadcrumbs
½ small onion, peeled and grated
½ teaspoon dried sage
1 large egg yolk (sizes 1, 2), beaten
salt
freshly ground black pepper
2 tablespoons oil
Sweet and sour sauce:
1×400 g (14 oz) can apricot halves in syrup
2 tablespoons cornflour
4 tablespoons soy sauce
4 tablespoons tomato relish
150 ml (¼ pint) light meat stock
1 small green pepper, cored, seeded and chopped
1 small red pepper, cored, seeded and chopped
2 slices fresh ginger root, peeled and chopped

Preparation time: 20 minutes
Cooking time: about 30 minutes

1. Mix the pork with the breadcrumbs, onion, sage and egg yolk, blending well. Add salt and pepper to taste. Shape into about 24 small balls.
2. Heat the oil in a deep, heavy-based frying pan. Add the pork balls and fry over a gentle heat for about 15 minutes, turning occasionally. Remove and drain on paper towels.
3. Meanwhile for the sauce, drain the apricots and mix the syrup with the cornflour in a pan. Add the soy sauce, tomato relish and stock. Bring to the boil, stirring constantly.
4. Lower the heat, add the peppers and ginger and simmer gently for 5 minutes.
5. Add the pork balls, coating them generously with the sauce and simmer gently for about 5 minutes, stirring frequently.
6. Slice the apricots and add to the pork mixture, mixing carefully. Taste and adjust the seasoning if necessary. Serve at once with boiled rice or a beansprout and mushroom salad.

> You can make a delicious crunchy mushroom and beansprout salad by tossing 175 g (6 oz) beansprouts and 100 g (4 oz) sliced button mushrooms in a dressing made by whisking 3 tablespoons olive oil with 4 tablespoons fresh orange juice, 1 tablespoon finely grated lemon rind and salt and pepper to taste.

Summer time pork pot; Sweet and sour pork balls, with a mushroom and bean sprout salad

CHORIZO AND CHILLI CON CARNE

3 tablespoons oil
2 onions, peeled and chopped
1 garlic clove, peeled and crushed
450 g (1 lb) lean minced beef
2 teaspoons dried oregano
1 teaspoon ground cumin
1 teaspoon chilli powder
1 tablespoon paprika pepper
salt
freshly ground black pepper
1×400 g (14 oz) can tomatoes
150 ml (¼ pint) beef stock
175 g (6 oz) chorizo sausage, skinned and cut into
   bite-sized pieces
1×432 g (15¼ oz) can red kidney beans, drained

Preparation time: 15 minutes
Cooking time: about 35-45 minutes

This is a speedy but extra tasty version of the classic chilli con carne. It has a hot spicy taste that comes not only from the chilli powder used but also from the chorizo sausage. Spanish chorizo sausages can be bought at most good delicatessens and are easily recognisable by their bright red colour. They are pork sausages flavoured with hot red pepper. If you find them difficult to buy, use any continental-type cured sausage with a hot spicy flavour.

1. Heat the oil in a large pan. Add the onions and garlic and fry for 5-10 minutes until lightly browned.
2. Add the beef and cook for about 10 minutes until lightly browned. Stir in the oregano, cumin, chilli powder, paprika and salt and pepper to taste. Cook over a moderate heat for 2-3 minutes.
3. Coarsely chop the tomatoes and add to the beef mixture with the tomato juice and beef stock. Cook, uncovered, over a moderate heat for about 10-15 minutes. Ⓐ Ⓕ
4. Stir in the chorizo sausage and beans and cook for a further 5 minutes.
5. Serve hot with boiled rice or crisp tortilla or corn crackers.

Ⓐ Chorizo and chilli con carne can be prepared a day in advance to stage 3, if liked. Chill until required. Reheat gently until hot, add the chorizo sausage and beans and complete the cooking as above.
Ⓕ Freeze for up to 3 months. Place from frozen in a saucepan and heat gently for 10-15 minutes until thawed and hot. Add the chorizo sausage and beans and complete the cooking as above.

CARBONADE OF BEEF

Serves 6
50 g (2 oz) butter or beef dripping
100 g (4 oz) back bacon, rinded and diced
450 g (1 lb) onions, peeled and sliced
1 garlic clove, peeled and crushed
1 kg (2 lb) braising steak, cubed
2 tablespoons plain flour
1 teaspoon brown sugar
1 tablespoon red wine vinegar
600 ml (1 pint) dark ale or stout
1 bouquet garni
1 strip orange peel
salt
freshly ground black pepper
grated nutmeg
225 g (8 oz) small button mushrooms
To garnish:
150 ml (¼ pint) soured cream (optional)
chopped fresh parsley

Preparation time: 20 minutes
Cooking time: 2½-3 hours
Oven: 150°C, 300°F, Gas Mark 2

1. Melt the butter or dripping in a flameproof casserole. Add the bacon and cook until crisp and golden. Remove and reserve.
2. Add the onions and garlic to the pan juices. Fry over a moderate heat until golden. Remove with a slotted spoon and reserve.
3. Add the beef to the pan juices and brown on all sides. Remove and reserve.
4. Add the flour to the pan juices and cook for 1 minute. Add the sugar and wine vinegar and cook until dark brown. Gradually add the ale or stout, blending well.
5. Add the bacon, onion mixture, beef, bouquet garni, orange peel and salt, pepper and nutmeg to taste. Place, covered, in a preheated oven and cook for 2 hours. F
6. Remove and discard the bouquet garni. Add the mushrooms, stirring well to blend. Cover and cook for a further 10-15 minutes. Serve hot, topped with swirls of the soured cream and parsley, with jacket potatoes or rice.

F Freeze up to 3 months. Thaw overnight in the refrigerator or for 6-8 hours at room temperature. Reheat gently on top of the cooker for 10 minutes. Add the mushrooms and cook for a further 10-15 minutes. Serve topped with swirls of the soured cream and parsley.

NAVARIN OF LAMB WITH HERBY CHOUX BUNS

Serves 5
50 g (2 oz) butter
225 g (8 oz) button onions, peeled
750 g (1½ lb) middle neck of lamb, cut into
    serving-sized pieces
40 g (1½ oz) seasoned flour
600 ml (1 pint) light meat stock
3 tablespoons tomato purée
1 garlic clove, peeled and crushed (optional)
1 bouquet garni
salt
freshly ground black pepper
450 g (1 lb) small new potatoes, peeled or scrubbed
225 g (8 oz) baby carrots, peeled or scrubbed
225 g (8 oz) baby turnips, peeled
100 g (4 oz) shelled peas
Herby choux buns:
150 ml (¼ pint) water
50 g (2 oz) butter
75 g (3 oz) plain flour
2 eggs, beaten
25 g (1 oz) mature Cheddar cheese, grated
½ teaspoon dried mixed herbs

Preparation time: 25 minutes
Cooking time: 1½ hours
Oven: 220°C, 425°F, Gas Mark 7;
then: 180°C, 350°F, Gas Mark 4

1. Melt the butter in a large flameproof casserole. Add the onions and fry gently for about 8 minutes until golden. Remove and set aside.
2. Add the meat and brown on all sides over a moderate heat. Remove and set aside.
3. Add the flour to the pan juices, blending well and cook for 1 minute. Gradually add the stock, stirring well. Bring to the boil, add the tomato purée, garlic if used, bouquet garni and salt and pepper to taste.
4. Add the meat, onions, potatoes, carrots and turnips and cook over a gentle heat for 30 minutes.
5. Meanwhile for the herby choux buns, place the water in a saucepan with the butter and heat gently until the butter melts. Bring to the boil. Sift the flour with a pinch of salt and add, all at once, to the butter and water mixture. Beat quickly to form a smooth choux paste. Cool until warm.
6. Gradually add the eggs, beating well to blend. Add the cheese, herbs and salt and pepper to taste. Spoon into a piping bag fitted with a large plain nozzle.
7. Stir the peas into the casserole. Pipe choux buns around the edge of the dish. Place, uncovered, in a preheated oven and cook for 20 minutes. Reduce the oven temperature and cook for a further 10 minutes.

Carbonade of beef; Navarin of lamb with herby choux buns

MEATBALLS GREEK STYLE

3 slices white or brown bread, crusts removed
750 g (1½ lb) minced lamb
1 onion, peeled and finely choped
1 garlic clove, peeled and crushed
1 teaspoon finely chopped fresh thyme
salt
freshly ground black pepper
Sauce:
3 egg yolks
3-4 tablespoons lemon juice
150 ml (¼ pint) water
To garnish:
shredded crisp lettuce
slices of lemon

Preparation time: 20 minutes
Cooking time: 30 minutes

1. Soak the bread in a little cold water then squeeze to remove any excess moisture. Place in a mixing bowl and blend with the lamb, onion, garlic, thyme and salt and pepper to taste. With wet hands, form into about 25-30 small balls about the size of a walnut.
2. Bring a saucepan of lightly salted water to the boil. Add the meatballs and cook over a gentle heat for about 20 minutes. Drain on paper towels.
3. Meanwhile for the sauce, beat the egg yolks in the top of a double saucepan or bowl standing in a saucepan of hot water until foamy. Add the lemon juice, water and salt and pepper to taste. Cook, whisking constantly, over a gentle heat until the sauce has thickened slightly.
4. Add the meatballs to the sauce to coat. Heat through gently before serving on a bed of shredded lettuce. Garnish with slices of lemon and serve with a tomato and onion side salad.

INDEX